In the Company of Fiber Artists

Creative Inspiration for Rigid Heddle Weavers

Tamara Poff

ISBN 978-0-9984590-2-8

Tucson, Arizona 85737

www.poffstudio.com

Layout and Design: Tamara Poff

Photography and Art Direction: Jill Greenop

Editor: Mikaela Koncija

Technical Editor: Lynn Lee

Yarn weight symbols, standard body measurements, and project levels source: Craft Yarn Council's www.yarnstandards.com

This book is dedicated to my mother for fostering a lifelong addiction to fiber art and to all moms and other teachers who ever shared their passion for creating. There you go, Mom. I finally wrote one for you!

I would also like to gratefully acknowledge the contribution of each of my beautiful models: Taelor Steen, Berlin Wright, Jordanna Riccitelli, Ashley Milhizer, and Alix Booms.

Contents

"Creativity is contagious. Pass it on."-Albert Einstein

Patterns

Sari Wrapped Skirt Bundle from Darn Good Yarn

Foreward

Tamara and I met like with most great relationships - on the internet. What made our introduction to each other different than most was that we were both on a path to maintain the integrity of the fiber arts community. It was from this that we understood our community of makers and artists continually needed a voice and proponents to tell our stories and bring us all in closer.

When I started my award-winning yarn company 13 years ago, I realized quickly that my raison d'être was to create a company that was a conduit for sustainable employment for as many people as it could touch. From artisans in India to fiber artists in the United States, my job is to link globally-sourced, unique products to the community of colorful people that use them with a people and earth-friendly motive.

As I've watched the industry evolve, I've been honestly astonished that the footholds of sourcing origin and historical connection haven't taken place as it has in other industries. I often like to use the example that you can probably go into your local supermarket and find "the green aisle." You know, it's the one where you can get fairly-traded coffee, gluten-free snacks, and organic juice. But in our crafting big-box stores, even down to our smaller retailers, that story for us just isn't being told as effectively as it could be accomplished.

This is precisely why Tamara's book is so important. Making and fiber art is a critical part to who we are as humans. It is almost as essential as our food. It's been around in some form since we realized we needed to wear clothing. Its evolution has been handed down just like cherished recipes. As the speed of our lives continues to increase, it's in our crafts that we settle back into a place of balance and calm.

Tamara has dedicated her life's work to education and fine arts. In this book, she expertly curated a collection of artists that bring with them their histories. Think about it, each piece we make ties back to our human roots. It's a beautiful tribute that ties us to a community through every pass of the yarn. You truly weave yourself into the human fabric.

When I source yarn for my company, I always think about what project it will be used for. Will it be used to make a gift? Will it be used for a utilitarian piece that gets used every day? It's a fun game to play, but I also take to heart how important the love that goes into how it starts to where it ends. It plays a beautiful role as a quality ingredient. But it's up to you. It's up to you to take a big breath and get connected to that boundless place. We all have the ability to tap into that deep, innate, and human part of ourselves. Turn off the external noise, the social medias, and anything else that can scare you away. Just for a little bit! You can rely on your internal voice to come out and express itself. It's part of you.

When a book like this comes along, it excites me because it encourages me that there are more rich stories out there of people who are drawing connections from their lives and bringing it to their medium. And what a treat that it is then taught and shared with us, so we can make it our own. Thank you, Tamara, for this delightful journey.

Peace, love, and keep crafting,

Nicole Snow
Founder + CEO
Darn Good Yarn Inc

Photo by Matthew Lancaster
Waco, TX

Introduction

"The only art I'll ever study is stuff that I can steal from"-David Bowie

As I write, we find ourselves in a world on lockdown from a coronavirus pandemic amidst the rise of socio-political chaos. There is no more critical time to find that which unites us as fiber lovers.

As a child, my mother longed for the sister she never had. She ended up with four daughters instead, filling that void and giving me three wonderful, crafty sisters to whom I am eternally and gratefully connected.

As crafters, we are all like siblings, connected with a common thread to a global community to which we can respond. Although the patterns are for rigid heddle weavers, anyone inspired to bring forth something new with their hands can find motivation here and respond to the call to add our imprint to that community.

Contrary to the notion that creativity is a "gift" given to the elite few, every maker is an artist. Don't think you are creative? Chances are, you have already been creative many times today. You may have called upon your creativity when you figured out what to wear, or you pulled together a meal limited by ingredients on hand, or you rearranged your workspace to suit you. Survival itself has required you to be creative.

Ok, some people do start with a greater sensitivity to color or design, but anyone can grow that imaginative self. First, know that you are creative by nature, then practice idea generation methods like those in this book. Further, accept that you are allowed to be influenced by others.

To this end, I've enlisted the following artists, notable for their mark on the history of fiber craft.

In chapter 1, Juliet Martin will share how she conquers "creative purgatory" with the start of each piece.

In chapter 2, Carol Leigh Brack-Kaiser highlights how working with others has helped make her business and her life successful.

Jane Dunnewold has made a career out of teaching artists and crafters to take their work to new heights. In chapter 3, she gives us ideas on how to stretch our imagination.

Knitting designer, Cornelia Tuttle Hamilton, gives us insight into how she has stayed true to herself to develop successful, sought-after patterns (chapter 4).

Share the love of color and the creative life with indie dyer, Tracey Schuh, in chapter 5.

Mona Muhammad (chapter 6) is a prolific innovator in the world of crochet. She reveals how she consistently creates beautiful and stylish wearables.

Chapter 7 features Lawrence Peters, a man with an eye for design who excels at the fine art of floor loom weaving along with the fine art of caring about others by giving back.

In chapter 8, Eco-fashion creator, Sue Burns, opens the door to using up discarded or unused pieces with her groundbreaking success in upcycled design.

In chapter 9, I leave you with the idea of thinking big about how your efforts can help change the world.

To each of the artists, I give my heartfelt thanks and admiration. I have learned much from them in the process of interviewing, and I'm thrilled to present them to you. I hope their influence will guide you toward your own successes and spur your continued exploration.

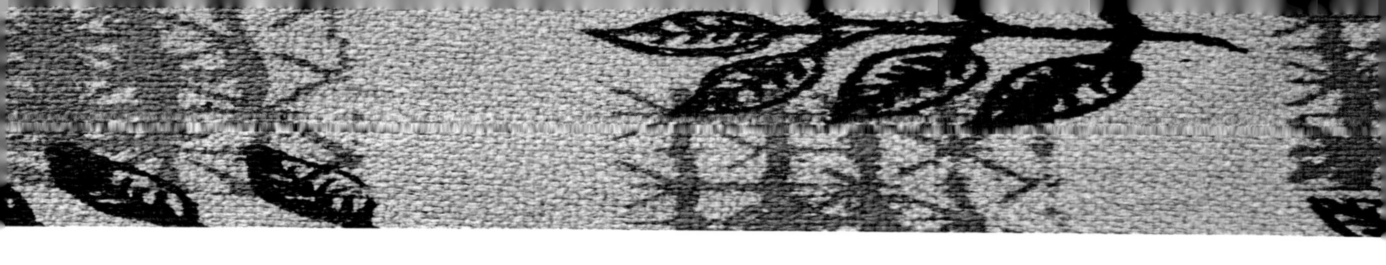

Warping and Weaving

I will guide you with direct warping rather than ask you to invest in a warping board. However, if you have limited space, you may want to get familiar with indirect warping on a board. You can learn this from YouTube. My books assume that you already know the basics of dressing the loom and plain weave. If not, you have YouTube, online courses, manuals, and local yarn shops to get a solid foundation. My teaching site, weavingwithpoffstudio.com, is one way to establish these skills.

With yarn quantities and warp length estimates, I allow for tying onto the front with a half knot and a bow rather than alternative knotting options. Not only does it reserve 6-7" of fringe where applicable, but I can easily adjust the tension later by untying and retightening the bow as needed.

My charts and diagrams are slightly different than the graphical representations handed down to us by our floor loom weaving cousins. Since very few of the hundreds of rigid heddle students I've taught come with that background, I sought to simplify the language as explained here.

Charts for warping

	6x			
20		20	Black
	4		Contrast

like the one at left, can be read from the right or the left coinciding with your dominant hand. This chart shows the number of ends (unless otherwise noted) that you will draw through the reed as you start from the back apron rod. Remember, every loop is two ends.

In our example: If you are direct warping from the right, facing the back of the loom, tie on to the rod at the right side and draw 10 loops through consecutive slots to make 20 ends. This will be the color Black as the green box indicates. Next, proceeding left, draw 4 ends (2 loops) of Contrast yarn. The grey box over the top of the 2 colors we just completed indicates 6 repeats of the sequence outlined in bold. You'll finish with 20 ends (10 loops) of Black.

NOTE-when you change yarns, always tie to the back apron rod (not yarn to yarn). Allowing alternating threads to travel past no more than one loop without cutting and tying off to the rod prevents excess crossing that can restrict the opening of the shed.

Charts for weaving

Contrast	Black
	20
4	

like the one at right, are typically read from the top down.

The names over the top indicate the yarn selection. This chart tells you to weave 20 picks of Black, then 4 picks of Contrast color. The pattern will tell you how often to repeat or reverse a sequence.

These charts are meant to abbreviate steps and are not a pictorial representation of the loom (unlike diagrams that follow).

Diagrams

Alternatively, there are times when the sequence for warp is a little more detailed, and a diagram of your reed is more useful. The following chart (A) is meant to look like the yarn passing through the reed.

A

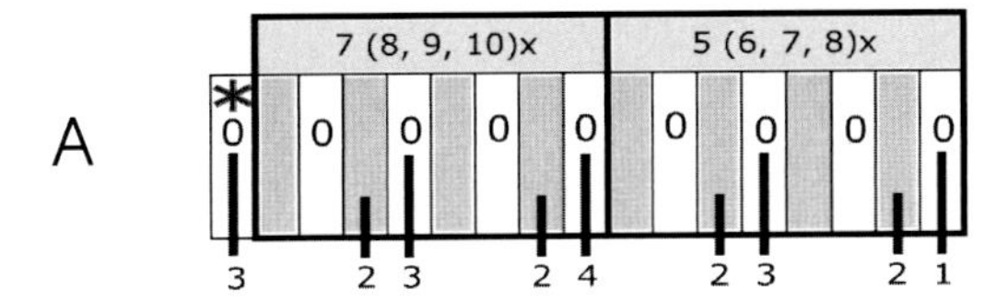

The vertical shaded bars are slots, and the white bars with holes are the heddles. The solid vertical lines are the yarns entering either the slot or the hole when we draw them through. If there is no line in that slot or hole, skip it as you draw loops. I follow A with a second chart for sleying the reed as shown below (B), so you can see how each slot and hole gets filled.

B

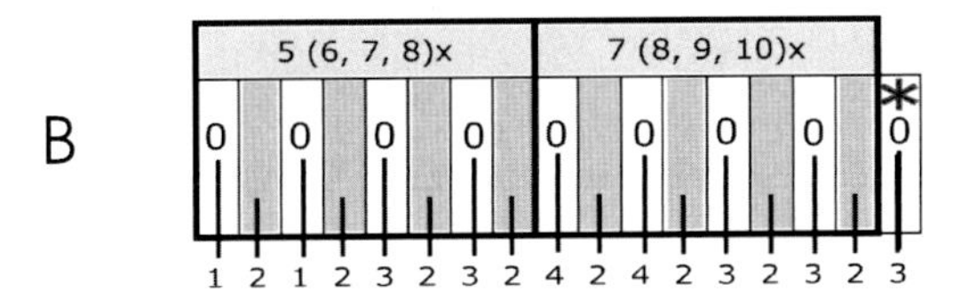

Note that B is the reverse of A. That's because you are facing the front of the loom in this step. Yarns are labeled 1, 2, 3, 4 here. Where specific color changes are involved, rather than yarn types, I color code the vertical bars instead. The green bar across the top will indicate the number of repeats for each section outlined in bold. Changes for each size are given in brackets.

Detailed descriptions of the use of these diagrams are given in each pattern. I will refer to loops as being "drawn" for A. In the next step (separating the loops to fill in the empty slots or holes), I refer to this action as "sleying."

Pick-up Patterns

When a pattern calls for the use of a pick-up stick for a textured weave of warp or weft floats, there are directions for setting one or two sticks. There will be steps to follow to change the heddle, and it is presumed, not written, that you will throw the shuttle each time.

If the float goes to the edge, there is always at least one edge where you have to wrap the selvage thread with your shuttle, or the weft will miss that end and create a gap there. Where this occurs varies depending on how you warped the loom and set the sticks. Once you discover this, it will show up in the same place each time. This is called managing the edges.

Some of the patterns in this book are written to border the floats with plain weave so you won't need to manage the edges.

Headers & Footers

You will need to start by weaving a header with scrap yarn every time to spread the warp evenly. Therefore, I won't repeat that in the patterns. Just know that your header should be just enough to get your warp even across. Using a scrap yarn that is the same gauge as your weft can be important to avoid a wavy header that keeps you from getting your best start. I abandoned torn plastic bags for headers a long time ago for this reason.

A footer is specified frequently in my designs. This is just scrap weaving for 6 -10 picks once a piece is woven. It is done when you are finishing with no fringe. It will protect the woven edge until you can get it machine stitched.

Wet Finishing

Washing is a must to get most woven pieces to look and feel their best.

It is critical to secure the woven edges by raw finishing on a sewing machine (see p. 18) if you haven't already knotted or hemstitched by hand. Wet finish all pieces before sewing them together.

I save tail and fringe trimming until after wet finishing and drying. Tails tend to poke their little heads out after washing, needing retrimming. However, I do cut long tails down to about 1" (cm) prior so they don't catch in the wash. One exception: I trim beginning and ending tails flush on the loom because they get in the way of sewing or tying fringe.

Before sewing, If using the typical polyester/cotton seam binding, it should also be washed. I find that it shrinks about 6% in length.

I prefer a no-rinse wash like Soak or Eucalon for its conditioning qualities and because you save a step by taking the fabric from suds to drying. I generally fill a plastic tub with about a teaspoon of soap and enough water to submerge my pieces.

Cotton and linen fabrics will hang onto wrinkles if left to dry. Pressing while still damp can improve them.

Wet Finishing Method One

Using tepid (room temperature) water, place the fabric in the soapy water, swish it gently, and then soak for 15 - 20 minutes.

I skip the soaking for hand dyes to preserve their color. You may want to try Shout® Color Catcher Dye-Trapping Sheets touted for retaining color where color bleed might be a problem. Most products for this purpose have some toxicity. Dharma Trading Company promotes their Professional Textile Detergent as more environmentally friendly for color retention. This is something you should trial on scarp fabric first.

Remove the fabric from the water, squeeze gently (no wringing), then place it flat onto a clean towel, roll it up, and press it firmly to squeeze out excess water.

For larger pieces, I sometimes use my washer's spin cycle to remove excess water and dry flat.

If your yarn label suggests, and you have a strong and stable fabric, you may run the pieces through the gentle cycle of your washer and tumble dry low. Using a mesh laundry bag can be helpful. I may use the machine for synthetics, rayon, cotton, or linen rather than animal fibers. For these protein fibers, I usually want to control the amount of fulling by using method two.

Wet Finishing Method Two - Fulling

Animal fibers achieve their potential for beauty and stability by fulling. This causes the tiny hairs of the strand to bloom to varying degrees depending upon agitation.

Using just enough tepid, soapy water, submerge and knead the fabric (like it was a loaf of bread) against the bottom of the basin for a one to three minutes. Some prefer warm or hot water to do the job, but you can accomplish this effect either way. Hot water may cause more shrinkage. Check the texture of the fabric to see if it has the bloom desired. You can run your fingernail from underneath along the cloth to see if it is stable - that the threads are not shifting where you might poke your finger through. Remove from the water as written in bold above and dry flat.

I recommend washing by hand rather than machine so you can control the bloom and avoid felting.

Wet Finishing Method Three - Shocking

Mohair (especially the fuzzy kind) loves a lot of open space for beautiful results. This may mean the fabric is fragile with unstable threads until it hits the wash, so handle with care.

Using soap and water as hot as your hands can stand (rubber gloves are a good idea), submerge the mohair fabric and soak for 15-20 minutes - no agitation. Remove and gently squeeze out the excess water as instructed in bold at the top on p. 12 and dry flat. The hot water causes the mohair fibers (and the wool to some extent) to fluff outward and cling together.

Yarn Substitutions

Good yarns come and go based upon marketability. Manufacturers generally introduce a new line twice a year and some of our favorites may be discontinued to make room.

Getting to know what yarns work on different size reeds and the properties of the fiber is expertise gained through experience and study. My 2nd book, *Color and Texture for the Rigid Heddle Loom,* is a deep dive into this subject.

Just about the time you get comfortable with your yarn choices, those yarns can be gone forever.

The website, yarnsub.com, provides an excellent tool for finding equivalent yarns for substitution. Regardless, we will always have those wonderful elements of surprise and experimentation as a part of our study. Don't be afraid to change reed sizes if your fabric isn't working out as you begin. I have a video for how to do that on YouTube, "Rescues for Rigid Heddle Weavers."

Yarn Weights & Gauges

Rigid heddle looms give us the unique opportunity to explore a vast range of beautiful knitting yarns. Therefore, I refer often to the Craft Yarn Council knitting and crochet gauges for selection. I've provided a clip of their chart below for yarns used in this book.

Weaving yarns are quite useful as well, but won't (alone) give us the full results possible with our looms.

Weaving yarn weights commonly useful to our looms are labeled 3/2, 5/2, and 8/2 and correspond to #3 (DK), #1 (Sock, fingering), and #0 (lace), respectively.

Categories of yarn, gauge ranges, and recommended needle and hook sizes

Yarn Weight Symbol & Category Names	0 LACE	1 SUPER FINE	2 FINE	3 LIGHT	4 MEDIUM	5 BULKY	6 SUPER BULKY	7 JUMBO
Type of Yarns in Category	Fingering, 10 count crochet thread	Sock, Fingering, Baby	Sport, Baby	DK, Light Worsted	Worsted, Afghan, Aran	Chunky, Craft, Rug	Bulky, Roving	Jumbo, Roving
Knit Gauge Range* in Stockinette Stitch to 4 inches	33–40** sts	27–32 sts	23–26 sts	21–24 sts	16–20 sts	12–15 sts	7–11 sts	6 sts and fewer
Recommended Needle in Metric Size Range	1.5–2.25 mm	2.25–3.25 mm	3.25–3.75 mm	3.75–4.5 mm	4.5–5.5 mm	5.5–8 mm	8–12.75 mm	12.75 mm and larger
Recommended Needle U.S. Size Range	000 to 1	1 to 3	3 to 5	5 to 7	7 to 9	9 to 11	11 to 17	17 and larger

Getting "Gauge"

The sett, or epi, is the number of warp ends per inch, which is the same as the reed dent size. The ppi is the number of picks per inch that I recommend in a pattern. I refer to the epi and ppi as the density of the weave. It is a good idea to pay attention to this number given at the beginning of each instruction to get the intended weave structure. Close (1-2 picks off) is good enough here. If your ppi is substantially different, your yarn substitution may be a problem, or you may be beating too hard or too light.

Watch for fabric instability. If your beat too lightly, your fabric will shift in an undesirable way. Likewise it may be weft dominant and stiff if you beat too hard - not what we want in wearable fabric.

If you are new to this, check ppi frequently by applying a tape measure to your weaving and counting the picks.

Supplemental Weaving Tools:

A simple hair pick is useful for beating weft into place when the reed won't do the job well. Some of the special techniques here will require this.

Fringe Twister
As a fan of wild and free fringe, I don't do a lot of twisting, but you might. If you do like this look, as in the Trila Shawl, p. 88 you will definitely want a twisting device.

Testing the Warp

This step is easy to forget when selecting warp yarn. Your choice must hold up to a certain amount of tension, whereas weft choices can be anything that will roll around the front beam.

Hold the yarn at points about 12" (30 cm) apart between index finger and thumb and pull steadily to simulate loom tension. If it pulls apart easily, it's a fail.

Also - don't forget the abrasion test. Rub a piece of your warp on the edge of a table. If it gets significantly fuzzy, or pills, or falls apart, it may do this as it passes through the reed and create problems. Sometimes this occurs with a slub yarn where the thread that makes the slub texture loosens and builds up behind the reed, compromising the warp.

I had a little trouble with this at the end of my weaving using the Berocco Quinoa that I love. (See the warp curling below) It was not significant enough to stop me from pushing the limits a little. I just did my best to smooth the bunched strands out and finish. It was well worth it.

If this occurs early in the weaving that may be a bigger problem. The abrasion test can save you some headaches.

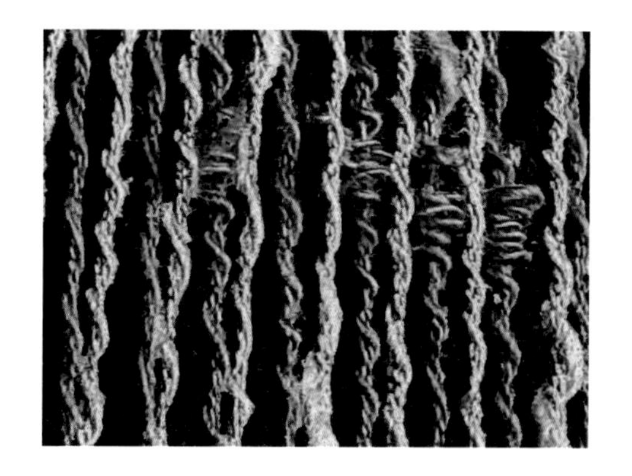

Definitions & Abbreviations

Apron Rods – are the rods attached with strings or plastic ties to front and back beams. Your warp ends attach to apron rods.

Beam - This is the cross member at front and at back of the loom. Your warp and fabric roll over these beams.

Cm - centimeter

Dent - reed size as in 8, 10, or 12 dent - referring to the epi of a reed

Ends - the vertical threads placed on the loom

Epi - ends per inch

Fell Line - is the last pick woven. The goal is a straight fell line except when working to make shapes as in tapestry weaving.

Gm - grams

Heddle - This is a vertical piece (usually plastic on the rigid heddle loom) with a hole that warp passes through. It is common to substitute the word heddle for reed.

Hole - the opening in a heddle

In - inches

K - knit

L - long

M - meters

P - purl

Pick - one pass of weft through the shed

Ppi - picks per inch

Reed - the loom accessory that holds heddles

SSK - Slip 2 stitches as if to knit. Place the left-hand needle in front of the stitches just slipped and knit 2 together.

Sts - stitches (for knitting instructions)

Shed - the opening created by moving the heddle up and down

Slot - the space between heddles

W - wide

Yds - yards

Garment Ease & Fit

When you produce functional and wearable items, you get a sense for the lengths and widths suitable for your body. For example, a 55" (140 cm) scarf may work for you for a single wrap around the neck, whereas 72" (183 cm) could be your minimum for the "cowboy" (double around the neck) wrap. Baby blankets size nicely at a minimum of 36" (91.5 cm) square. Your favorite fit for a top may be 20-21" (51-54 cm) to hit at high hip, or you might feel better with a longer length at 23" (59 cm). Do you like a close fit, or is loose better for you? If you have something in your possession that already works well, then you can make note of the dimensions of that item as you create something new.

Being aware of your size issues will give you better results to make the changes you need, adding to or subtracting from the warp length, width, and weaving length of a pattern. I will give you the amount of ease intended (extra width around the chest) where applicable so you can make these decisions.

Since we all weave differently (and due to yarn substitutions), you may have slightly different results than suggested in the pattern. Pay close attention to measurements as you proceed through weaving, washing, and assembly where it matters. You may want to plan ahead and increase or decrease weaving width or length or make adjustments in seam allowances.

Also, despite our best efforts at a straight fell line as we weave, it is not uncommon to find that one side of your woven rectangle is longer than the other. Being aware of this and making adjustments in hems and seams can be important to the finish quality of certain pieces.

Sewing Handwovens

So you've made a few scarves, placemats, and other rectangles. You're ready to try some new shapes, but the fear of machine stitching that beautiful fabric has you frozen.

The first time I put my handwoven work under the needle of a sewing machine, it took me about 5 minutes to jam that heavy, 1970s machine into a state beyond reasonable repair. My apologies to my mother-in-law, who so generously donated it to me.

Since that time, I've sewn miles and miles of handwoven fabric. I'll give you some of the best things I've learned here.

Miscellaneous

Sewing handwoven cloth from the rigid heddle is a little different than traditional sewing with commercially made fabric. We have selvages that we consider finished edges, so we seldom interface anything - yay! Seams can be bulky, and fitting to the body's angles can be challenging, so we have to get tricky to make our results appealing. I'll be showing you ways to cut angles with painter's tape as your guide for this purpose.

Also, holding the fabric at the back and front of the piece helps to move it along as you sew. However, don't force it or you could disturb your machine's timing and stretch the fabric.

The older I get, the less I finish hems or bind seams. This is not because I am getting lazy, but I'm becoming more and more convinced that the rawness of our work is a part of its beauty.

Finally, before we dive in, I have a confession to make. I am nowhere near the capability of a professional seamstress, but I can sew a pretty good straight line and zigzag stitch fairly accurately. This is all you need to strive for to sew my patterns.

Equipment

Sewing Machine: I replaced that poor, battered machine with an entry-level BrotherBL9, and six years later, I'm still using the same simple model. It doesn't do anything fancy but is of good quality, lighter on the fabric, and has a free arm option to get into hard to reach places.

Accessories (photos at right): A walking foot can be very handy. I use mine extensively. Most of the time we are sewing through heavy thicknesses. The walking foot can help you travel over textured, thick, or layered fabric without getting buried in the landscape of a weave or skewing layers.

Check to see that the walking foot you buy is compatible with your machine. It's essential to install it correctly. The lever at the top either fits around the tightening screw with its little fork or over it if it is just a bar like the one shown at right.

A rotary cutter, metal straightedge, and self-healing mat can be obtained from sewing stores or online, are relatively inexpensive, and indispensable for cutting fringe accurately. Before I purchased these, I hung my fringe from the edge of a countertop and tried to trim straight across. Yeah, buy the cutter and mat.

You'll appreciate two types of good sharp scissors - larger ones for cutting warp and other big jobs, small ones (like embroiderers use) for cutting weft when unraveling, and for cutting tails. There are numerous handheld scissor sharpeners like my little yellow fish for under $10 on Amazon that work very well to keep scissors well-honed.

You'll need plenty of straight pins and some knit clips. Knit clips are great for putting garments together or connecting abutting pieces like blanket panels.

Needles

When I first learned to sew, I thought a machine needle lasted until I broke it - one size fits all. *Au contraire* - some suggest changing the needle after every three bobbin loads or 8 hours total sewing time.

You may have a hard time keeping track of that. I suggest keeping extra needles on hand in various sizes. If you have any doubts, compare the old needle to a new one to see if it looks dull or bent.

Regarding needle sizes, the packages should tell you what fabric weight is associated with each size. I work in the mid-range of available sizes - medium to heavyweight as follows:

No. 80/12 – Medium Fabrics
No. 90/14 – Medium (slightly heavier) Fabrics
No. 100/16 – Heavyweight Fabrics

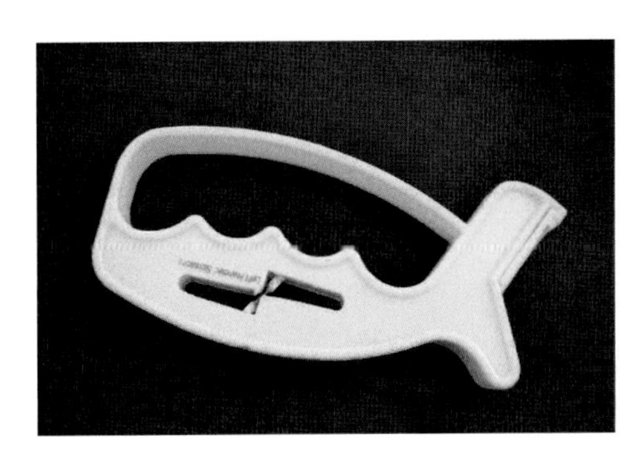

Choosing a Stitch Length

I choose between 2.5 mm and 4mm stitch lengths. If your machine has a broader range than mine and you want to go there, try it.

Most of the time, I am using a 2.5 mm for finer fabrics and a 3 mm stitch for heavier cloth when putting pieces together and sewing zigzag. If you are insecure at any time about how your pieces will fit, I strongly suggest you sew with a 4mm and no backstitching until you are confident. I've gritted my teeth over enough ripping out of a nearly indelible seam to backstitch carefully. You can always stitch over your original machine basting when you are sure of yourself.

Thread

I use all-purpose thread most of the time. Polyester is best for wearables. Sometimes it helps to use a coordinating but slightly different color. A perfect match to the fabric often disappears deep into the weaving.

Where a raw finish edge will be showing, I match the thread more closely.

Raw Finish

You'll be doing a lot of this if you are going to cut woven fabric. A walking foot can be useful here to avoid stretching edges.

One of my mentors swears by a double straight line of stitching to secure the fabric before cutting, and that may work for you. It does not work for me, however. Maybe I make too many demands on my cloth?

Anyway, here's my raw finish hem: I consider the weft pick at the very edge of a piece to be sacrificial. Aim at zigzag stitching across to link together the 2nd and 3rd pick from the edge. Adjust your stitch size to pierce or span those 2 picks. After the first row, turn, and sew another zigzag row either just inside or on top of your first row.

Fluff the cut ends gently to bring out the waste, and trim close to your stitching. If you stray a bit in sewing and accidentally catch that first pick, it will blend in vs. the scrap yarn that may border it. Sometimes, where the raw finish is supposed to show, you will want to go back later and retrim any missed ends that sneak out on you.

While this is a very secure edge for most work, if you really test it, yes, you will be able to unravel the raw finished edge. In the rare times this may happen while working, take the piece back to your machine and double zigzag over the damage.

So there is no confusion; when I write "raw finish all ends," I am (of course) referring to the ends that will be cut, not the selvages.

I hear mixed reviews about using a serger on handwoven fabric from the seamstresses who own them. Buying one can be an expensive and tricky path for the occasional sewer. If you already own one, and want to try it for woven edges, gather some scraps and practice first.

Tips for Stretchy Fabrics

To avoid wavy edges when raw finishing stretchy fabrics, choose the right needle size and make sure it is sharp. Guide the fabric gently - don't tug on it as you sew.

Some weavers use a fusible tape to stabilize edges (that aren't intended to show) and seams. Keep in mind that this can add bulk and impair drape, so consider it carefully. Shoulder seams may be a good place for this.

Seams

I generally use 1/2" (1.5 cm) seams where the allowances will be pressed open, 5/8" (1.6 cm) seams where a lot is going on in the allowance (like gathering), and 1/4" (.5 cm) seams where the allowances will be sewn together and pressed to the side. Lastly, I love the "skinny seam" with just 2 warp ends of allowance at the selvage. It makes a great transition where a seam opens to a neckline. I will give you the recommended allowances in the steps of each pattern.

Seaming to Match Stripes

This can be challenging since weaving density can vary as we work. I aim for a good match (not a perfect one) for this reason.

Use your long basting stitch with no backstitching until you get it where you want it. Here is my chosen method for matching. As shown on the next page, place pins horizontally at each stripe along the top thread of the stripe to be matched. Look at the piece on the other side to see that the pin lines up with the corresponding thread. I keep these pins just slightly away from (but close to) the sewing line to avoid problems associated with hitting the pin with the machine needle.

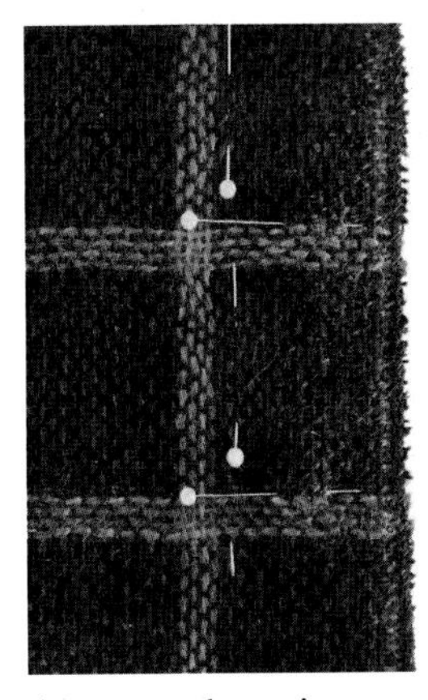

Place vertical pins to stabilize between the stripes and sew using a walking foot.

Back Stitching & Stay Stitching

Once you are clear about what you are doing, backstitching is important to secure ends. If you are starting at the edge of a piece, it can be very helpful to start 1/2" (1.5 cm) inward from the edge, stitch back to the edge, then go forward. This can give your machine momentum to move forward and is especially important if your fabric is fragile, where the machine might chew it up as you start.

It's also important to reinforce any edges where seams open up to a neckline or an open underarm area like the shrug on p. 122. We put a certain amount of stress on those areas in the wearing that can tug on and stretch yarn there, so I'll recommend a little bit of stay stitching around those vulnerable areas. As shown below, I double stitch about 1/2" on each side of the opening.

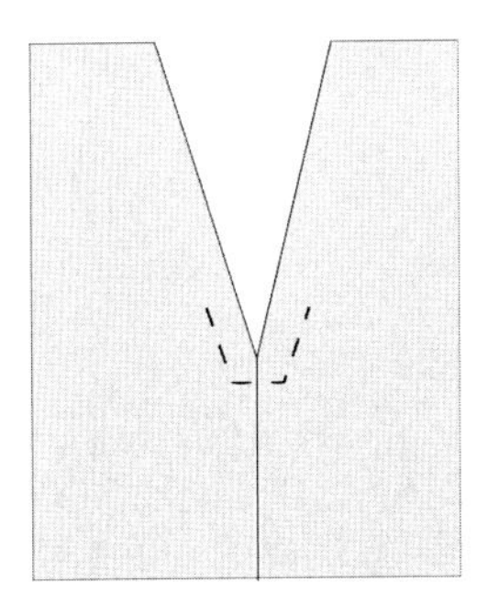

Pressing

Some of my weavers are avid knitters who are shy about pressing because it will flatten the knitted stitch.

Woven fabric is not so fragile in this way, and it often wrinkles where knitting seldom does.

With most fabrics, use moderate pressure and rely on steam as needed.

With cotton and linen, press while still wet from the wash since these fabrics tend to hold onto wrinkles. You can be more aggressive with these.

With smooth silk, pressing brings out the shine and flexibility of the piece. I use a low setting, no steam (that might stain), and press firmly for this fiber.

For rayons (bamboo, Tencel), use a light pressure and steam press on a wool setting if needed.

Some suggest wetting wool with a spray bottle of water to protect the fiber (or press it while still damp from the wash).

If your yarn contains any synthetic material, be sure to use a pressing cloth. Acrylics, nylons, and polyesters can all melt under high heat.

Fit

I want to restate how important it is to get a good grasp on your desired ease and fit before you get deep into making a garment (p. 15). Be sure to check your work as you go, and improvise with seam allowances as needed. If pieces are too small, you might resolve this by adding a little crochet, knitting, or woven gussets to join.

...and Practice, Practice, Practice

Consider adding a few inches to your warp and weave a scrap piece so you can try your technique before you commit.

Chapter 1

"If you're not doing some things that are crazy, then you're doing the wrong things."

-Larry Page

"Because everything has the same life, life cannot be measured by a yardstick. It is this individuality that makes everything meaningful and the uniqueness of each thread that creates the tapestry of life."

-Misao Jo

Taking that first step toward creating new and exciting work on your rigid heddle starts with trying something that goes against our all too comfortable routine. I love the challenge inspired by our first artist as you read onward. Throughout this book, you will find other little challenges to take your weaving to a higher level and help you find your own voice in the creative work you do.

I took a class in Saori weaving from Laura Lundy in Tucson in 2019. Laura is an instructor certified by the Japanese studio, Saori Nomori (The Saori Forest). This experience took me beyond my usual range and led to the patterns I created for this chapter. You will find that they are loosely written. Along with free-form weaving comes free will, leaving you, the maker, in charge of the creative decisions.

Saori weaving is a movement founded in 1969 by Misao Jo (also founder of Saori Nomori) and continued today by her family in Osaka, Japan. It is the method of "no rules" weaving, directed toward finding your authentic self and connecting with others. Raw edges, lumps and bumps, mismatches, and mistakes – all are embraced.

I introduce just a few of the techniques used in the art of Saori. With my instructor's blessings, we refer to the teaching in the patterns here as weaving in the Saori style rather than weaving Saori. It is just a glimpse into that which is certified and promoted by Saori Nomori. More about this magnificent art form and its creator can be found at www.saoriglobal.com.

For many students of the rigid heddle, there remains a fear of messing up our precious work. That fear can hold us back from our best work, or worse, stop our practice altogether. Talking with Juliet Martin for this chapter reminded me of what needs to be done when perfectionism or coveting our work compromises our results.

Juliet Martin

I went on a mission in search of someone with a unique interpretation of the Saori style. I was delighted to discover the ever passionate, ever whimsical textile artist, Juliet Martin.

She began her career doing web-based art pieces recognized around the world by such icons as SIGGRAPH and The New York Times.

In the nine years since her involvement with the fiber arts community, she has had solo shows at Ivy Brown Gallery, New York City; Chashama, New York City; Living Room, St. Peter's Church, New York City; Sumei Center, Newark, NJ; Creative Arts Workshop, New Haven, CT; Garrison Art Center, Garrison, NY; Artworks Gallery, Trenton, NJ; and Saori Kaikan Gallery, Osaka, Japan.

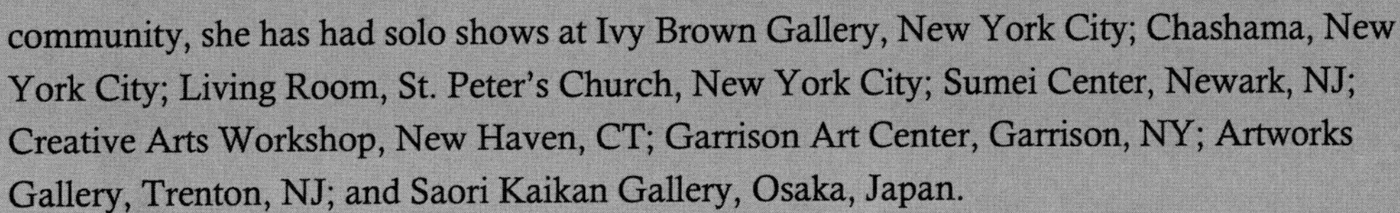

Juliet turns the medium of Saori around, deconstructing and recontextualizing it to convey meaning that reaches out to the viewer in humorous, yet thought-provoking ways.

Find out more about Juliet Martin at www.julietmartin.com.

Sitting Room on Monday from
Household Items Remind Me of You
17" x 17"

What are you looking for when you begin a new piece?

For me, when I'm starting a new project, my husband and I call it weaving purgatory. When I'm in between two places, it's so painful and so difficult. I have to say to myself, "Just hold on. Just keep going." My most recent series is called *Household Items Remind Me of You.* The way that came about was, I had finished this show that had to do with faces and eyes and interactions. A lot of my pieces have to do with person-on-person relationships.

I was sketching a lot, and I noticed I was drawing coffee tables and wine glasses. I realized, with the coronavirus, I haven't been seeing any people, so all of my relationships are with these household items. It's just me and my husband in our apartment. He would go out to empty the trash, and all of a sudden, I'm like, "Oh my god! I'm alone. I'm never going to see him again. All I have is my sofa." So I sort of joked that these were my new relationships. I wouldn't have figured that out if I wasn't sketching. It's about intimate relationships that are replacing our normal human contact.

What led you to connect your high-tech background with a high-touch medium?

I was an art and math major in college. More recently, in 1994, I was in grad school for computer art. Even at that point, I was trying to deconstruct the medium. As computers go, they were very emotional, very touchy-feely. I tried to take the medium and turn it inside out.

I ended up teaching at a university where the program really beat me down. I felt like I had to touch something. I felt like I had to move beyond the screen. I had always said on the screen, "Can you see me through the computer?" That was sort of an endless question.

So when I got overwhelmed with the impersonal nature of that program and, almost again, feeling so alone, this made me lean toward trying something more physical. I brought along a lot of the same ideas from, "Can you see me through the computer?" to what I call satirical memoirs.

Toothpaste **from** ***Household Items Remind Me of You***
10" x 11"

I love your whimsical approach to communicating your very personal point of view. What experiences in your life might have contributed to your sense of humor and irony?

I have bipolar disorder. For about 20 years, my medication was totally off, so I dealt with depression for about 50% of my life, from about 18-38. I bring that up, not as a part of self-pity or disability, but it forced me to make a joke about it. The only way I was going to get by was to try to look at the bright side. It became a way of life.

I still find that when I'm using somewhat serious topics and can approach them with a little humor, it not only makes me feel better, but I think it allows a connection to the work. It's like an open door. You're going to see it at first, and it's going to be funny, but then you have this access, then you look a little further, and you realize, "Oh, this is about gender inequality" or whatever. It seems to work quite well in conveying a message.

No, you can't always look on the bright side, and no, you can't always make a joke, but sometimes you really need to. It's a little bit about saving one's self.

Tell me about your connection to Saori weaving.

I went to work with Kenzo, one of the sons of the woman who created Saori. A friend and I went to Osaka for a week. I have to say that I was a little, "Oh, I know everything. What can he teach me?" I had been doing Saori for about four years, so I figured I would just go in there and tear it apart. Kenzo was so funny. He decided to call me "Crazy," and that was my nickname. He taught me all these things. I don't know how much I actually use those techniques, but there's just so much.

The American painter, Grant Wood, said, "All the really good ideas I ever had came to me while I was milking a cow." What non-art activities fuel your creative expression?

This is tough because I work all the time. I get up; I read art philosophy in the morning. Then I draw, and then I start weaving. I work out at 4:30. I cook dinner at 6:30. I feel like it's not the activity so much as it is the process.

One thing I do is spinning. I know that spinning can be considered an art form, but when I spin, I focus on the process. I almost force myself to not make aesthetic decisions. I just want to be moving and to be meditating. Sometimes I end up with something nice, but sometimes I don't.

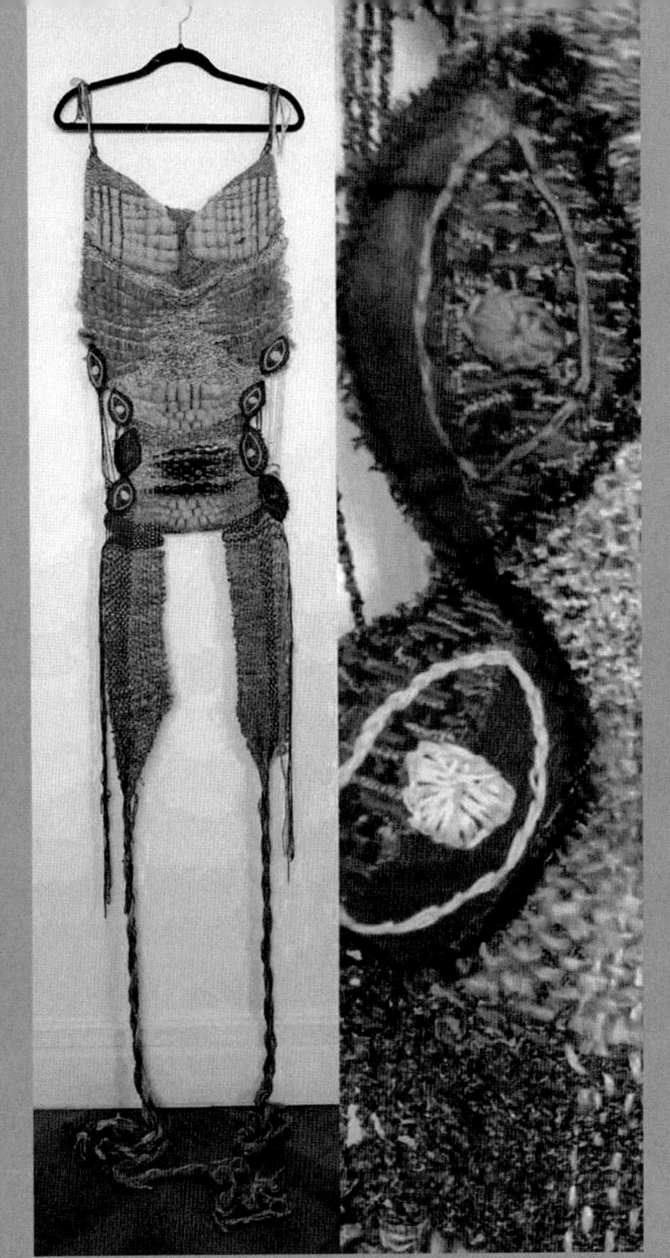

Lime Green **(and detail) from** ***My Eyes are Down Here***
72" x 18"

Do you have a mentor, and what are your thoughts about mentors?

I did ceramics for a while, and then I moved into weaving. For a year, I lived in Singapore. I found a ceramics center that was really just a roof with four posts and a bunch of wheels. There was this very tiny man, Singaporean, who would throw these vessels that were massive. Once when he was not there, I left him a post-it note on his wheel, "Can you teach me, and I will pay you?" The next day I went there, and he came up to me and said, "You will not pay me. You will learn from me. I will teach you." I was like, "Yeah!"

It turns out that he was one of the top ceramists in Southeast Asia. He chose to work with me because I didn't know who he was - because I liked the pure form of his work.

But, I'm sure you have heard of these teaching methods where they make you do 100 mugs all the

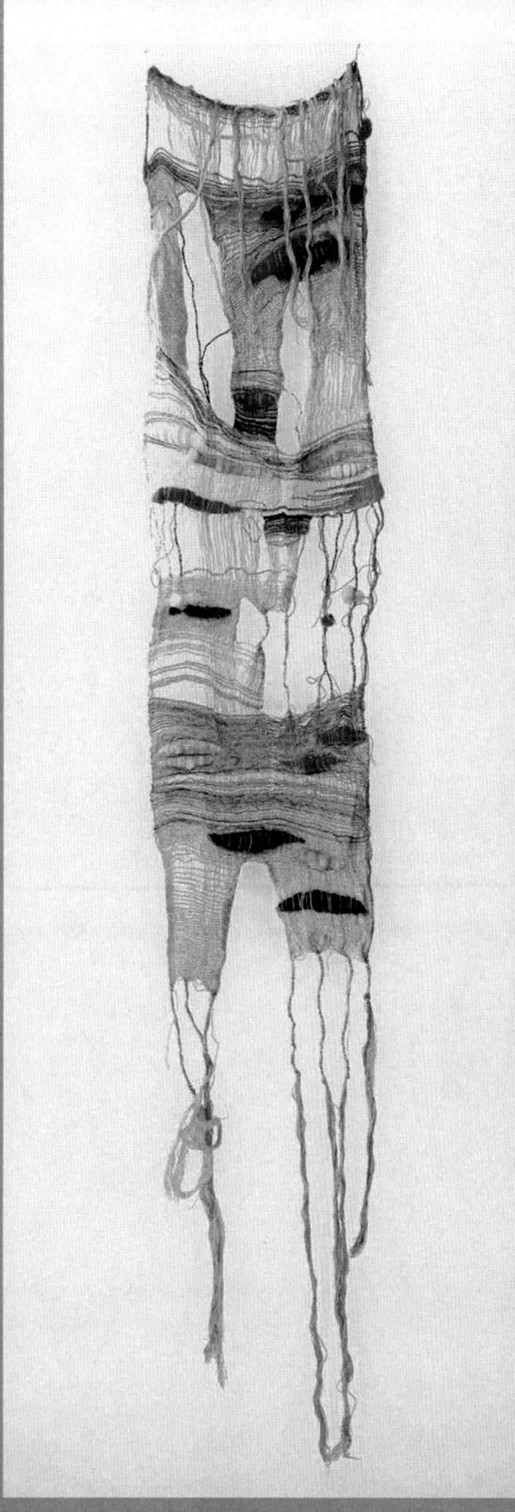

***The European* from *Men I Have Known* 40" x 14"**

same. So, I'm making these mugs, and he's telling me how to make it the same as the one before and the one after. Then I graduated. I was able to decorate a cup, I showed it to him, and he said, "This is not art. You are not an artist. Go back and do it again!"

He took this place as a mentor, and I really feel like he took advantage of it and beat me down as opposed to making me excel. I love the idea of a mentor, but that position is so dangerous. There is a loaded misconception of what a mentor should be and what a mentor is. I feel like the scale can be tilted if your mentor is so driven by their own vision that you don't have space for yourself.

What do you want your viewer to gain from your work?

I will take a topic that I think is important, as I mentioned before, like gender inequality, sexism in the workplace, emotional turmoil, and give people access through humor. I did a collection called *Men I Have Known*. That's a funny title, but it's also presenting how women are put into their place because of how they look or what they are willing to do.

I did one called *My Eyes are Down Here*. It's funny. It's goofy, but at the same time, I'm trying to communicate a message. I had an opening for that show, and I had a young man, probably 21 years old, say to me, "Oh my god. I never understood what it was like before for women. Now that I see your show…" So that was very meaningful to me. Shows are great and selling stuff is great – fabulous – but that connection, like with that young man, is what gives me fulfillment.

I did a show called *You Don't Look Crazy,* and a friend of mine who is also bipolar said, "You said exactly how I feel." That was just unbelievable. Making those connections is important for the viewer, and it's important for me. The weaving, the humor, the illustrations, they're like a gateway.

Tell me a story of a time when you were inspired by something outside your world.

My Mom invited me to see the Picasso sculpture exhibit at the Museum of Modern Art. I didn't want to go

***I'm Not a Puppet* from *You Don't Look Crazy* 19" x 33" x 7"**

because he was a sexist, and he was a jerk. My Mom said, "Just go." I was so mad because I loved it. I thought, "He's so good. This is killing me. I can't believe it!" So, I went home and decided, "I'm going to make a series called *I'm Not Picasso*." I started creating all these female figures, and that's where my series, *My Eyes are Down Here*, came from. I was trying to take his approach to sculpture and turn it into my own thing. Still, I'm not fond of Picasso, but that is one of the ways I came to my work.

What advice would you lend to a weaver struggling to find their own direction with their craft?

Cut, cut, cut. Precious is bad. I feel like if I do something that I love it so much, it usually means that it's too precious, and I have to cut it up. For a while, what I was doing was weaving fabric, and then I would put it in a pot of boiling water for 20 minutes and then put it in the dryer on high. Everything would be so different. They turned into these wonderful things that I never could have planned.

I was giving a workshop, and I told everyone to bring something they really loved, maybe not finished. When we got there, I was like, "All right, we're going to cut this up and make something new." It forces you to reconsider what you are doing. It forces you to think about what you want, and I think it makes a huge difference. Taking it somewhere different, you end up with a solution that you wouldn't have had normally.

So, what is next for you and your art?

I'm enjoying writing more and more and getting back to painting. This last group of household items has been, for me, bringing together my love of drawing, my love of painting, weaving, and writing. It makes me want to continue to put those together in unique ways. I feel like I made great strides with this last collection. The one before that, there was writing, but it wasn't incorporated as much.

I don't see myself exploring book arts so much, but I do want to pursue more storytelling in my work.

Exercise: Cut, Shape, Explore

We can create so many beautiful things from our handwoven goods if we shed the fear of cutting into our work to reconstruct. Before you move on to the patterns, this fun and revealing exercise will prepare you to tear into that cloth and expose some creativity.

This one is not a pattern. I'll give you some ideas on how I came up with "The Man Purse," but the intent here is that you will make this project your own. Will it become a freestanding sculpture, a pillow, something to wear, something to hang on the wall? You will decide.

Suggested Equipment and Materials

- Sewing machine and coordinating thread
- Your handwoven fabric
- Scrap yarn
- Pins and tapestry needle
- Note pad and pen for brainstorming
- Scraps, discarded toys, yard debris, household implements, etc. that might lend to your creation

I found some plastic golf balls and a couple of small rubber bands to hold them to make the eyes. For the strap, I appropriated one of my husband's silk ties. To make my project a proper handbag, I used high quality felt to craft the liner.

When I am a designer writing patterns, my goal is to create pieces (mostly wearables) accessible to my weavers while working away from the traditional.

When I am a painter, I paint about women's issues, social justice, and the examination of stereotypes.

To make this exercise personal, I approached it with my painter's brain to create *The Man Purse*. It has found a place hanging on my studio wall to remind me to avoid taking myself too seriously.

This is dedicated to my husband, who is a good sport about holding my purse for me in public but won't use a purple suitcase because he thinks that is a girl color. Love you, babe.

What I Did

With Juliet Martin's advice, I went into my studio to find a piece of fabric that I had woven and loved. A big part of this exercise is to take a risk and let go of something you are holding close – an abandonment of ego to make your weaving stronger. You will find that cutting and sewing garments and accessories will be far less frightening after you do this.

I found this multi-texture, multi-color cowl made from novelty yarns and handspun. I had no preconceived notion for the piece. I simply started thinking about how to repurpose the weaving. I stuffed some plastic golf balls in it, tossed it on the table, threw it in a decorative bowl, scrunched it, shaped it, pinned it, and hung it on the wall to look at it. In the process, I was thinking about both humor and content.

I thought about who I am as a weaver. Since I am not a sculptor, it occurred to me that I should make something to wear or an accessory. This scrunchy thing would become a handbag. Then I thought about what I am as a painter. This handbag would become a metaphor for questioning gender norms - a psychological portrait of masculine and feminine stereotypes. Above all, it would just be fun.

So I went to the sewing machine and zipped up a simple bag from the cowl with a front flap with plastic golf balls for eyeballs surrounded by small rubber bands to hold them in place.

I said to myself, "I have to put some effort into this to bring home some meaning that makes sacrificing my cowl worthwhile."

To complete the bag, I cut some high quality felt (purchased on etsy.com) to the bag body size and made a lining that I sewed on 3 sides and stitched in place around the top. I like to use felt for bag linings because it has a nice weight to it. Also, I can trim it to size and not have to fuss with hemming the edges.

I took some scrap yarn and a tapestry needle to sew simple pupils and eyebrows on the flap, keeping the expression neutral.

Furthering the man theme, I thought about using a man's belt for the strap, then eureka! I found the husband's tie to be just the thing to sew on at each side. My husband is very forgiving.

Lastly, I cut some red handwoven scrap in the shape of a mouth. I hand-stitched around it and within it with more scrap yarn to form the smile.

The Man Purse

What Will You Do?

The Exercise

1. Consider who you are: Are you an artist, an embroiderer, a knitter, a crocheter, or a spinner? Perhaps you are a golfer, a fitness buff, an educator, a reader, a writer, or a homemaker?

2. Identify what you weave: Do you like to make decorative art, home goods, garments, functional pieces?

3. Weave or select something from your collection that makes you a little uncomfortable to deconstruct. This will be your foundation.

4. Write down all the possibilities you can think of to create something with steps 1 and 2 in mind. While you are doing this, manipulate the cloth into shapes that relate to your ideas. Maybe this could be a golf club cover, a kitchen towel, a placemat, a plant hanger, a framed piece for the wall, a center piece for your table, a book cover, a cape, or a toilet paper cover (my grandmother had one of those).

5. Gather items on hand or purchase things to incorporate into your idea. I got those used Barbie dolls on eBay.

6. Cut, cut, cut, sew, stitch, staple, or glue to make your design come to life. See p.16 for sewing advice.

There are no mistakes here. If you feel you have a mishap in the cutting and sewing, find a way to incorporate it (or even make it the focal point) in your message.

Don't stop at your first few changes. What can you do to bring more life to your piece?

Congratulations, you have now gone "beyond the rectangle," and we are just getting started. To commemorate your success, take photos, and send them to a friend OR post them to my Facebook page: Poff Studio. I would love to see your results!

This simple cowl will introduce you to just a few of the techniques of the Saori style.

Once you get the hang of it, you may want to try your hand at the similarly inspired sweater on p. 38.

Free-Form Cowl

How far can you go with "no mistakes" weaving? Start with a one-of-a-kind cowl woven to finish at 38" (96.5 cm) long. If you prefer a longer scarf, there is advice for this in the warp instructions.

The weaving techniques will be described in detail. Choose your favorite ones to repeat and alternate them as you go. Plain weave is used throughout to create inlays, shapes, and textural variations.

Finished Measurements approximately 10-1/2" (26.5 cm) W x 38" (96.5) cm L

Equipment

- Loom with at least 12" (30.5 cm) weaving width
- 8 dent reed
- At least 2 stick shuttles for main colors. I used 6 yarns, so it was helpful to have plastic yarn bobbins to hold small bits of yarn for the difference.
- Buttons as desired to embellish the surface. I used one 2" (5 cm) and three 1" (2-1/2 cm) coconut buttons.
- Tapestry needle to sew buttons on and join cowl

Warp

Interlacements ZigZag , 100% rayon in Brown, 8 oz = 500 yds (457 m). Uses 184 yds (168.5 m).

Weft

Chose 2 contrast colors of smooth dominant yarns for main 1 and main 2, and scraps of novelties, varied weights, and fabric.

For main colors, I used one ball each of DK weight Naturally Dyed Recycled Silk from Darn Good Yarn, 120 yds (110 m). Uses approximately 70 yds (64 m) of each. These provide a background for fancy yarn.

I used other small bits from Darn Good Yarn, including their Indian Brushstrokes printed ribbon and Herbal Dyed Silk Ribbon. I used a bulky cotton yarn and some glitzy eyelash/slub yarn from Trendsetter Sorbet– now discontinued but still around online. Substitute any glitzy eyelash yarn.

You can also go on etsy.com to find a variety of novelty yarn grab bags.

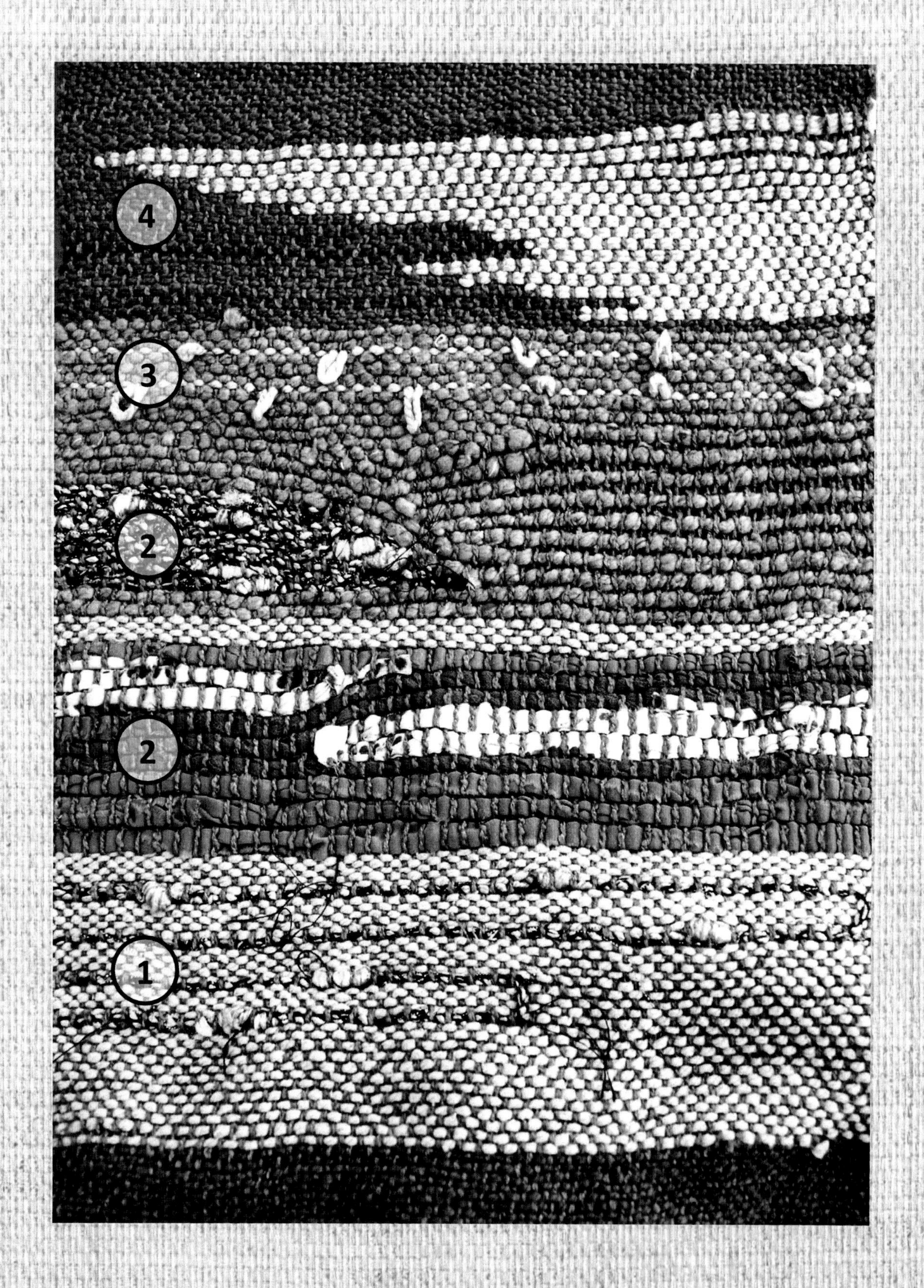
4
3
2
2
1

8 epi, ppi varies according to yarns used.

Warp

12" (30.5 cm) W x 66" (167.5cm) L = (96 ends) with ZigZag. If you have extra yardage and want a scarf, decide how much longer you want it to be (finished). Grab your calculator and divide this number by 0.9. Add the resulting inches (cm) to your warp length.

If you would like to figure the extra yarn amount needed for warp, multiply that last number x 96 (ends) to get inches (cm). Then divide by 36 for inches to yards or 100 for centimeters to meters.

Weave

for a total of 42" (107 cm) or longer if you added warp for the scarf length.

My main color 1 is brown, and my main color 2 is cream.

I'll give you the weave type in the order I started this piece, but you can mix it up in any way you like. The special techniques are numbered to correspond to the photo at left and on p. 36. Practice each one. Then you will decide which ones are your favorite to repeat at intervals to the desired length.

Weave tails in as you go, or when you finish, or leave them hanging for a different effect. We won't worry about nice, even selvages here as the multiple yarn gauges and weave variations make that unattainable. Additionally, the rawness and asymmetry of the work is a notable feature of this type of weaving.

I like to work with each technique for 3-5" (8 –13 cm), varying the length each time for variety.

To begin: Plain weave with your main color 1 for 5". Change to main color 2 and weave for 12 picks.

1. **Inlay** (running a pick of contrast yarn along with the main color weft): With a bobbin of eyelash yarn, starting from the left selvage, I placed a length of about 6" into the next shed, leaving the bobbin hanging out of the front of the fabric. Weave the next pick across with main 2 in the same shed, and then plain weave four picks with main 2. Carry the bobbin yarn upward and lay it into the next shed going back to the left selvage. Weave main color 2 across in the same shed, then weave 4 picks with it. Carry the bobbin yarn up the left edge and repeat the inlay, this time to the right and stopping about 1" before the right selvage. Repeat these steps staggering the endpoint as desired.

Here I changed to a brown ribbon to plain weave 4 picks.

2. **Tapestry shapes** (with ribbon and novelty fill): If you want to create your own ribbon from fabric, see the instructions that follow. To inlay the shape, I started from the right edge and wove back and forth to form an irregular area. Then I wove the contrasting ribbon around it. Use a hair pick, a fork, or handheld beater to beat the weft into place as you raise and lower the heddle to work back and forth. You can see the brown ribbon traveling around this shape in the photo at left. I created another shape to straighten my fell line and finished this section with 1 pick of brown ribbon.

How to Cut Ribbon from Fabric

Here is a simple method to make ribbon for weaving when you only need a small amount:

Fold your fabric along the shortest edge.

To make a continuous strip, starting in a bottom corner at the fold, cut about 1" (2.5 cm) wide along

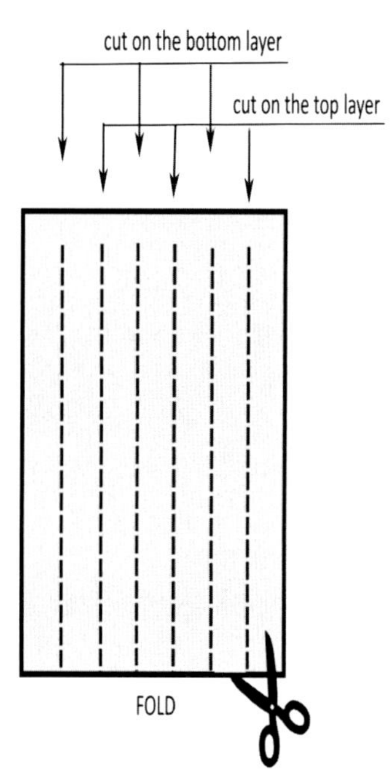

the fabric length to about 1" (2.5 cm) from the top across the fold. Now turn the folded cloth around and snip to the first cut on the top layer only. Then finish the 2nd cut on the bottom layer only. Alternate, completing every other cut between the top and bottom layers across, and you have a continuous strand. When you beat the ribbon as weft, the connections will blend in.

Change to main color 2 and weave 4 picks. Change to the bulky cotton to weave 2 picks.

3 **Pulling up loops**: Throw 1 pick of main 2. Pull up small loops at intervals, beat, and change the shed. Weave 3 picks in bulky cotton, throw another pick of main 2, and repeat the loops.

They will be more interesting if you stagger the location of the loops.

Weave 2 picks in bulky cotton. If you are ready to move on to #4, change to main color 1 and weave 1 pick.

4 **Two-color interlock (Figure 1, next page) - also called clasped weft:** Place the ball of main color 2 on the floor on the opposite side of where your shuttle is. Pass the shuttle through the shed to the other side. Lay the tail from the ball over the shuttle yarn. Without changing the shed, pull the shuttle back through to drag the ball thread into the shed with its tail hanging out the side. This puts two picks

in each shed. Pull one side against the other to decide where to drop the interlock point and to adjust the selvages. Beat, change the shed, and repeat, staggering the interlock point. The starting tail can be woven in later.

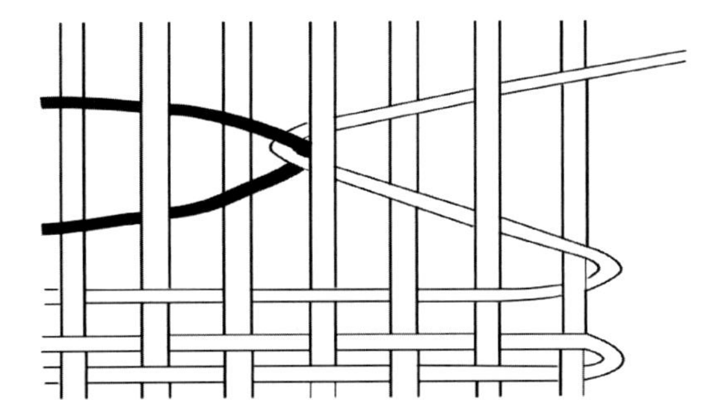

Figure 1-Two Color Interlock

Complete the desired length of two-color interlock (I did 3", 7.5 cm), then continue with main 1 in plain weave for 2" (5 cm).

5 **WWW: (Figure 2)** So-called because you will throw a pick, then stick your finger through the warp from above to pull that weft pick up and down to form a shape like a W (or multiple W's). When you beat it, you will get random dots as shown due to the excess weft in the shed.

I finished this section with 6 picks of main 1, changed to ribbon and wove 7 picks, then switched to main 2 and wove 9 picks plain.

6 **Knots: (Figure 3)** Wrap yarn around four fingers 4-5 times and cut at one end to create short strands of equal length. Holding the strands together, wrap them over 2 adjacent warp threads, and bring them up between the same 2 warp threads as shown. Trim the knots to the desired length.

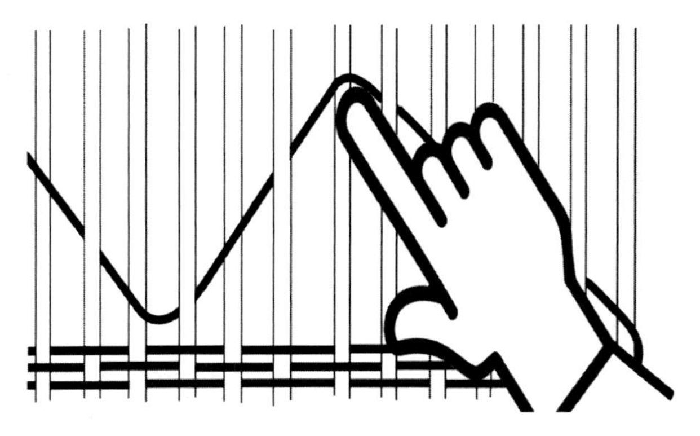

Figure 2 - WWW

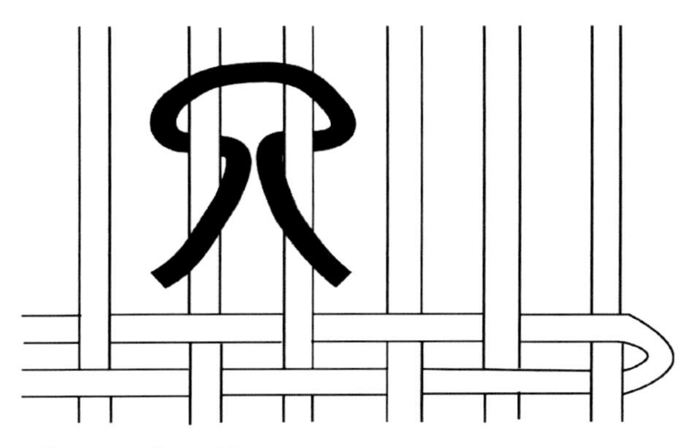

Figure 3 - Knots

Place knots at intervals across, pulling them down close to the last pick as you go. Continue in plain weave for at least 2 picks to lock the knots in place.

Alternate the techniques to finish at the desired length.

Finish

Cut from the loom tying 4 strand fringe tassels and wash according to method one, p. 12.

Using yarn and the tapestry needle, overlap and attach the ends of your cowl with a couple of stitches to wear as shown in the photo on p. 32. Apply decorative buttons as desired.

Saori style weaving on the body and a pick -up weave for the sleeves brings east and west together in this piece.

The knitted cuff is optional.

Winter in the Wood Sweater

Free-Form your way around the body of this design, woven side-to-side using the techniques from p. 34-37. This one was chosen for the 2020 "Seasons of the Smokies" Wearable Art Exhibit by the Handweaver's Guild of America. Now you can make your own.

True to the Saori style, I have left the bottom edges unhemmed for a natural, wavy line. The finished length given below is an average for this reason. This design has a cropped effect to hit at high hip and a loose 5-7" (12.5 - 18 cm) of ease at the bust. Finished measurements are given in Diagram 2, p. 42 if you wish to make adjustments.

	Small	Med	Large	X Large
To Fit Bust	32-34" 81.5-86.5 cm	36-38" 91.5-96.5cm	40-42" 101.5-106.5 cm	44-46" 112-117 cm
Finished Bust	39" 99 cm	43" 109 cm	47" 119.5 cm	51" 129.5 cm
Avg. Length	19-1/2" 49.5 cm	20" 51 cm	20-1/2" 52 cm	21" 53.5 cm

Equipment

- Loom with at least 25" (63.5 cm) weaving width.
- 12 dent reed
- At least 2 stick shuttles for main colors. It was helpful to have plastic yarn bobbins to hold small bits of yarn.
- 1 Pick-up stick to weave sleeves
- Sewing machine with coordinating thread
- Crochet hook, size D or E (3.25 or 3.5 mm) - optional for finishing the neckline
- US 4 (3.5mm), 32" (80 cm) circular needles or double points plus a stitch marker for optional cuffs

Yarns Used

This was a chance to use stash yarns on hand. I will make suggestions, but anything goes. You'll get a good drape if you choose viscose yarns for warp: rayon, bamboo, or Tencel (lyocell).

Body warp: 8/2, lace gauge, rayon - equivalent to Maurice Brassard 8/2 Tencel or Bamboo in a gold color for the warp. 5/2, fingering gauge, like the 5/2 Dragon Tale rayon from Earth Guild will also work. Uses 564 (608, 54, 709) yds, 516 (556, 598.5, 648.5) cm.

Body weft: I used 3 main colors, gray single ply handspun (approx. sport gauge), 5/2 Tencel in brown, and Dandoh Silk+ in Angora (76% raw silk, 24% cotton, 50 gm = 227 yds). For inlay accents, I used small quantities of 3 different novelty yarns (fur, glitter, tape) plus small amounts

(continued on p. 40)

of 3 colors (white, black, gray) wool roving. I also wove with a batik print, brown and black fabric. See p. 35-36 for how to cut fabric for weaving.

Sleeves: For warp, I used 5/2 Tencel in a brown color. Any fingering weight will work. 8/2 will not give the sleeves enough weight. Uses 265 (276, 290, 300) yds. For weft, I used the Dandoh Silk+. Uses 200 (213, 229, 245) yds.

You will warp 2 times as follows:

Warp Front & Back

23-1/2 (24, 24-1/2, 25)" , 59.5 (61, 62, 63.5) cm W, x 72 (76, 80, 85)", 183 (193, 203, 216) cm L = 282 (288, 294, 300) ends with 8/2 or 5/2 rayon. If you are warping the full width of your reed for the X Large, you will draw one loop to the outside of the reed.

Weave Front & Back

(make 2, 12 epi, ppi varies by yarn used) using the Saori style techniques from p. 34-37. You will weave the first piece for 23 (25, 27, 29-1/2)", 58.5 (63.5, 68.5, 75) cm, cut and tuck the weft tail, weave 2 pieces of contrasting scrap yarn to separate, then weave the 2nd piece of equal length.

I decided to forego the tapestry shapes in favor of two -color interlock, loops, knots, WWW, and inlay applied in a stairstep fashion. You can see photos of the full width of the front and back on p. 43.

I also used several single row pieces of roving (black, white, and gray) inlaid to add texture. If you pull the fibers out to taper to a point at each end of the roving, the ends will blend in well as you go.

In some places, I pulled up short loops of the roving to make a bauble effect. In other places, I overlapped 3 colors of roving in the same shed or wove several picks of black roving. Once again, the idea is to change what you are weaving every 3-5" (8 - 13 cm) and experiment.

When you have woven 2 pieces of equal length, separated by 2 picks of scrap yarn, weave a footer and raw finish all starting and ending edges before cutting the pieces apart, p. 18.

Warp Sleeves

14-1/2" (37 cm) W x 40 (41, 42, 43)", 101.5 (104, 106.5, 109) cm L = 174 ends with 5/2 Tencel.

Weave Sleeves

(make 2, 12 epi, 16 ppi) for a length of 15-1/2 (16-1/2, 17-3/4, 19)", 39.5 (42, 45, 48.5) cm with the pick-up pattern below.

I found that the Dandoh yarn and the pick-up weave created a little extra shrinkage (about 17% for length and 15% for width). I normally use 15% for width and 10% for length.

Set the pick-up stick by placing the reed in the down position. On the top row of threads behind the reed, *pass over 2 ends, pick up 2 ends. Repeat from * across ending over 2 ends. Push the pick-up stick to the back beam until you need it on step 5.

6 step pick-up weave: throw the shuttle for each of the following steps.

1. Heddle Up
2. Heddle Down
3. Heddle Up
4. Heddle Down
5. Heddle in neutral. Set the pick-up stick upright against the reed.
6. Heddle Down

When the first piece measures the length for your size, cut and tuck the weft tail, weave 2 picks of contrasting scrap yarn, then weave the 2nd piece identical to the first.

Weave a footer, cut from the loom, and raw finish all starting and ending edges. Cut the 2 pieces apart.

Finish

Wash according to method one on p. 12.

Shoulder seams and neck edges:

With right sides of the body pieces together, sew each shoulder seam leaving a 12" (30.5 cm) opening in the center for the neck opening. Use a minimum of 1/2" (1.5 cm) for the seam allowance. This edge will be a bit wavy, so the seam allowance will vary.

Press the shoulder seams open and front and back neck edge inward to match the shoulder seam allowance. Machine stitch 3/8" (1 cm) away from the neck opening edge, 1/2" (1.5 cm) beyond the beginning and end of that opening (see Diagram 1 below right for a view of the neckline from above laid flat).

Sleeve underarm seams: Weft floats on the front side are warp floats on the back. I chose the back side for my "right " side because I liked its subtlety. With right sides together, sew the raw finish edges of one sleeve together with 1/2" (1.5 cm) seam allowance. Press the seam allowance open. Repeat for the other sleeve. If you are not knitting the optional cuff, skip to "sew side seams." The sleeve edge will be a selvage. You may wish to turn a hem for a casing and thread elastic around the edge for a different effect.

Diagram 1

wrong side
neck opening
shoulder seam
stitich neck edge

If knitting the tapered cuff around the sleeve, it measures 1-1/2" (4 cm) long and, the gauge is approx. 22 sts/4" (10cm).

Use Dandoh Silk+ to start at the underarm seam, and pick up 68 (72, 78, 84) stitches around one edge of a sleeve, 2 warp ends inward from the selvage.

Place a marker for the start of the round. Work 4 rounds in K1, P1 rib.

Next round: *SSK, K1, P1. Repeat from * around. For large size, end with SSK. 51 (54, 58, 63) sts remaining.

Work K2, P1 around. For large size, end K1. Repeat the last round 3 more times.

Next round: *SSK, P1, K2, P1. Repeat from * around, ending:

SSK, P1 for small and X large

SSK, P1, K1 for large

Bind off the remaining 42 (45, 48, 52) sts and repeat for the other sleeve.

Sew the side seams: Measure the sleeve width now that the underarm seam is sewn. With body right sides together, mark an armhole opening matching the sleeve width from the shoulder down on each side with a pin. Sew the side seams from the pin to the bottom edge with a 1/2" seam allowance. Press the seams open.

Set in the sleeves: With the body still inside out and a sleeve turned right side out, set the sleeve into the armhole, matching the underarm seams (right sides are together). Sew around the armhole with a 1/2" (1.5 cm) seam allowance. Repeat for the other side.

If preferred, single crochet around the neck opening and your sweater is ready to wear - a one of a kind work of art!

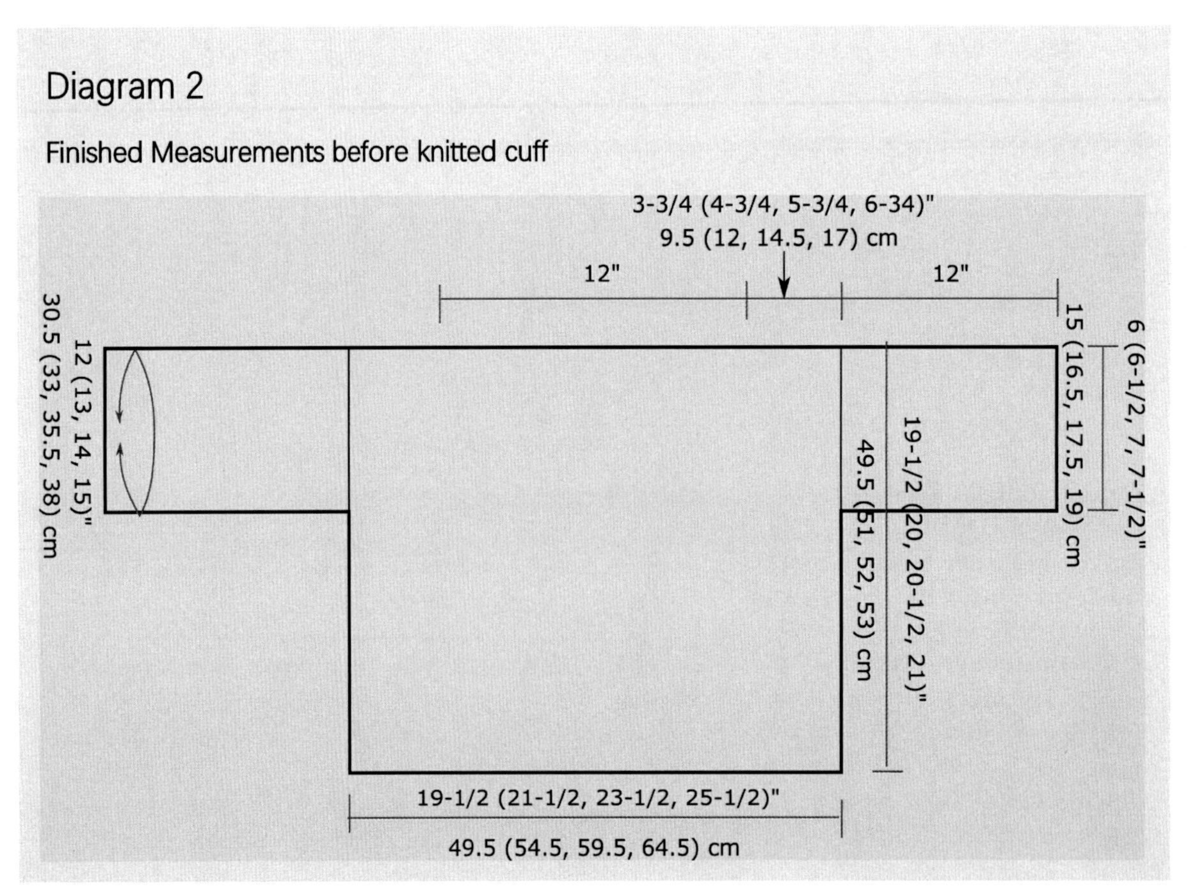

Close-Up View Across Each Side

The front and back of this loose-fit sweater are reversible.

Chapter 2

"Alone, we can do so little; together we can do so much."

-Helen Keller

"None of us is as smart as all of us."

-Ken Blanchard

I attended a demonstration by Carol Leigh Brack-Kaiser at the Handweaver's Guild of America's Convergence conference in 2018. I was so impressed by her stunning creations and enthusiasm for continuous strand weaving that I ended up buying one of her Mini Module kits. This contained 2 beautiful, handmade 6" continuous strand looms - a square and a triangle.

Like so many of my well-intentioned acquisitions, I let these wooden looms sit in the box for the next 2 years. I suddenly realized how fun it might be to embellish my regular weaving with the little woven pieces I aspired to create. These simple little squares I subsequently produced added a new twist to my rigid heddle designs.

Working at home, as I often do when writing and designing, means long stretches of solitude. As something of an introvert, I need this alone time for focus and productivity. Still, intermittent contact with a creative community is an essential element that balances my life. I achieve that balance through my art memberships and by teaching weaving from time-to-time.

Then there are the folks who get their creative juice by working daily with others. Our next artist has built a successful business surrounded by family and friends. She also travels and volunteers extensively to nurture her craft, as you will gather from her interview.

One key to your productivity as a crafter may be to consider which type of person you are, then seek out that level of community that enriches your own creative soul.

Are you satisfied with your level of human connection? On one end of the spectrum, do you need to carve out more time for yourself, or at the other end, would you benefit from more interaction?

You can add to your network through meetup groups and other like-minded memberships. Find them online (meetup.com). Or maybe you will join or start your own mastermind group (peer-to-peer mentoring alliances) for your creative work. Try youtube.com for advice on how to get one going or google mastermind groups for your area if interested.

Carol Leigh Brack-Kaiser

Carol Leigh Brack-Kaiser is the absolute authority on continuous strand weaving. No one has done more to expand the creative options available with this craft. For over 38 years, she has made her business, Carol Leigh's Specialities and Hillcreek Fiber Studio in Columbia, Missouri, a family affair, offering tools, dyes, and fibers for both weavers and spinners.

She has recruited husband, Dennis, to build smaller looms and tools. He's also the accountant and shipper. Son Carl builds large looms and other wooden tools, and daughter Rose is her professional photographer. Her daughter Bex has her own knitting business and promotes the family products.

Carol Leigh's ex, Phil, was their webmaster before he passed, a job now taken by grandson, Ben, her tech assistant.

Carol Leigh surely knows the meaning of Community as wc explorc in the following interview.

To learn more about her, Hill Creek Fiber Studio, and the products they provide, visit:

www.hillcreekfiberstudio.com.

What inspired you to take up craft for a living?

As a child, I had a potholder loom and sold potholders around the neighborhood. Later as a girl scout - they actually had a weaving badge back then - we had to create a rigid heddle loom from an old orange crate. I made the frame, hand-tied all the heddles, and wove two or three projects on it to get that weaving badge. So I have always had a fascination with threads going under and over threads.

Wedding Ring Quilt Pillow

I started college with a major in music, then sociology, then rehab counseling. With a marriage, a move from Iowa to Missouri, a family to raise, and my work schedule, It took me seventeen years to get my undergraduate degree.

When I finally got my degree in 1979, I took a class just for the fun of it - a spinning class at a craft studio on campus. My instructor was also working with natural dyes. She asked me to help her, so I did that for about three years. Then she stepped out, and I continued to do the master dyeing demonstrations for thirteen more years.

From there, I became infatuated with obtaining colors from nature. I had also taken a couple of weaving classes from a local weaving store at that time, so it all kind of came together.

I have always enjoyed spinning, weaving, and dyeing, so I decided, "Why not do it for a living?" I started in 1982 as Carol Leigh's Specialties as a part-time business. I had a macramé and candle making business by that name back in the '70s. By 1986, there were so many people asking me, "How do you do that?" so I set up a studio to teach spinning, weaving, and dyeing and added Hillcreek Fiber Studio to my business name.

...and what inspired you to take the deep dive into the continuous strand loom?

I took a class from Paula Simmons [i.e., author of *Spinning and Weaving with Wool*, Pacific Search Press, 1979, and many other books about wool and raising sheep]. She was teaching this class about weaving on table looms with our handspun yarn. Our host's husband had fashioned these triangle frame looms from broomstick handles. Paula had seen that idea at a Renaissance Festival. As one of the first two people who finished her class, I got to play on them and became fascinated with the concept. It was so easy to do and so portable. You don't have to thread a loom ahead of time. You can just jump right in.

In my research, this weaving method appears to have been practiced in England since the middle ages. Before that, it is likely that the Vikings brought a form of it with them.

I brought the idea home. My son, Carl, is a woodworker, so he started making triangle looms for us. People began asking for different sizes. He came up with an adjustable feature that adjusts from 7 feet down to 3-1/2 feet, and we wound up getting a patent on it. It allows you to put the woven pieces together in many different ways. We've got our loom in all 50 states and quite a few foreign countries as well.

Then people started asking us for different shapes, so Carl decided to create an adjustable square loom that matches up to each increment on the sides of the triangle loom.

When those long rectangular scarves started becoming so popular, Carl came up with an adjustable rectangular loom that is 7 feet long and adjusts to 25 different sizes where the length is some multiple of the sides.

When I was asked to teach a one-hour class at a knitting conference, Carl came up with the Mini-Mods because even our two-foot triangle loom was too big for this.

Your book, *Continuous Strand Weaving Method*, offers a huge variety of projects for your weavers, from beanies to bed covers. Give me a glimpse into how some of those designs came to be.

The book took me sixteen years to finish. Every time I finished a design, I'd think of six more, so it just kept going. People kept contributing to it, as you can see in the back of the book.

Two of my grandsons also contributed. One was six years old when he created a pouch from one of those little squares that he folded. He called it the Padawan Pouch. I had to have him repeat the name several times because I had no idea what he was talking about. He said, "Don't you watch Star Wars, Grandma? A Padawan is a Jedi apprentice." I said, "A who?"

My then twelve-year-old grandson came up with a bikini top for his girlfriend from two triangles from the Mini-Mod set. He did Inkle weaving for the band and sewed it all together. When it came time to give it to his girlfriend, he said, "Grandma, I don't think it's big enough!"

Panel Suit Vest and Skirt

Anyway, the first thing you need to do is get familiar with the process, and then you let your mind wander.

Your family members are deeply involved in so many aspects of your business. How has their feedback shaped your design work?

They've had creative ideas as well. My daughter Bex used to teach middle school science; then, she started to work for us as a merchandiser. She developed the knitting part of our business to the point where the knitting was taking over our weaving studio. In 2003, we decided she needed to open her own business.

That's when she started Hillcreek Yarn Shop, where she carries our products as well as knitting supplies. She's always been mathematically inclined, so being used to working with geometry, she was able to put things together for us. Also, the people working with her have been able to design for us. Little bits here and there is how things have come together.

My youngest daughter, Rose, is our photographer. When the book took so many years to put together, she said, "One more project, Mom, and I Quit!"

She came up with the Sling Bag in the back of the book using rag strips. It was something I never thought of. Putting those two triangles together to form automatic pockets was ingenious.

I feel so fortunate that so many people were interested in contributing to the book.

You've had three generations of family (and an ex-husband) working together at Hillcreek Fiber Studio. How have you made that work so well for so long?

Well, my husband and ex-husband got along just fine. When Phil was in need of a job, his expertise in technology was valuable to our business.

Everybody has their own unique skills. I'm blessed with having so many people with skills that I don't have. You can't do the whole thing by yourself.

What outside interests continue to drive your work?

As I'm inching toward retirement and not doing as many shows, one of my major interests is in plants and the outdoors. I've joined three different plant groups: an herb group, the Missouri Native Plant Group, and the Missouri Master Naturalist Group.

Our new tech guy lives about an hour and a half away in a county that used to be considered the hemp capital of Missouri back in the 1800s. He got me started raising hemp plants. So, I've got a "hemp plantation," and I've been spinning the fibers and using the leaves for dyes.

I've always had an interest in hemp. The Declaration of Independence was originally drafted on hemp paper. It lasts better than most paper from trees. Hemp has so many practical and environmentally beneficial uses - CBD oil for pain, hempcrete for building. You can even make tea out of the leaves.

I have had some really interesting experiences over the years studying on the Navajo reservation and in Turkey. I've been to Peru, Malaysia, and Oaxaca, where I've enjoyed working with other civilizations to learn their weaving, spinning, and dyeing skills.

In the last six years, I've also participated in WARP, which stands for Weave A Real Peace. Many of the members are fiber artists who work with indigenous communities throughout the world, helping them expand their economic base and revive historic weaving and dyeing practices. They have an annual meeting in different places each year to share their experiences.

How do you see current trends and influences affecting your business going forward?

Wool potholder weaving has become a very popular thing to do with people staying at home. Wool makes the most sense for these, as it is fire retardant and more insulative than cotton. They're natural-dyed wool, and we carry the natural dyes for them as well. There are a lot of back-to-basics things going on right now.

About 15 years ago, Harrisville stopped making the wool loops, but they allowed me to special order them, just for us, with a minimum of 100 lbs. and six months' lead time. I've reordered many times since.

My grandson put the potholders on our Etsy site, and those potholders have really taken off. They're about 1/3 of our business now. I consider myself as having come full circle – starting with potholders as a five-year-old child and now doing them again.

MU Stadium Blanket

Vincent & his Padawan Pouch

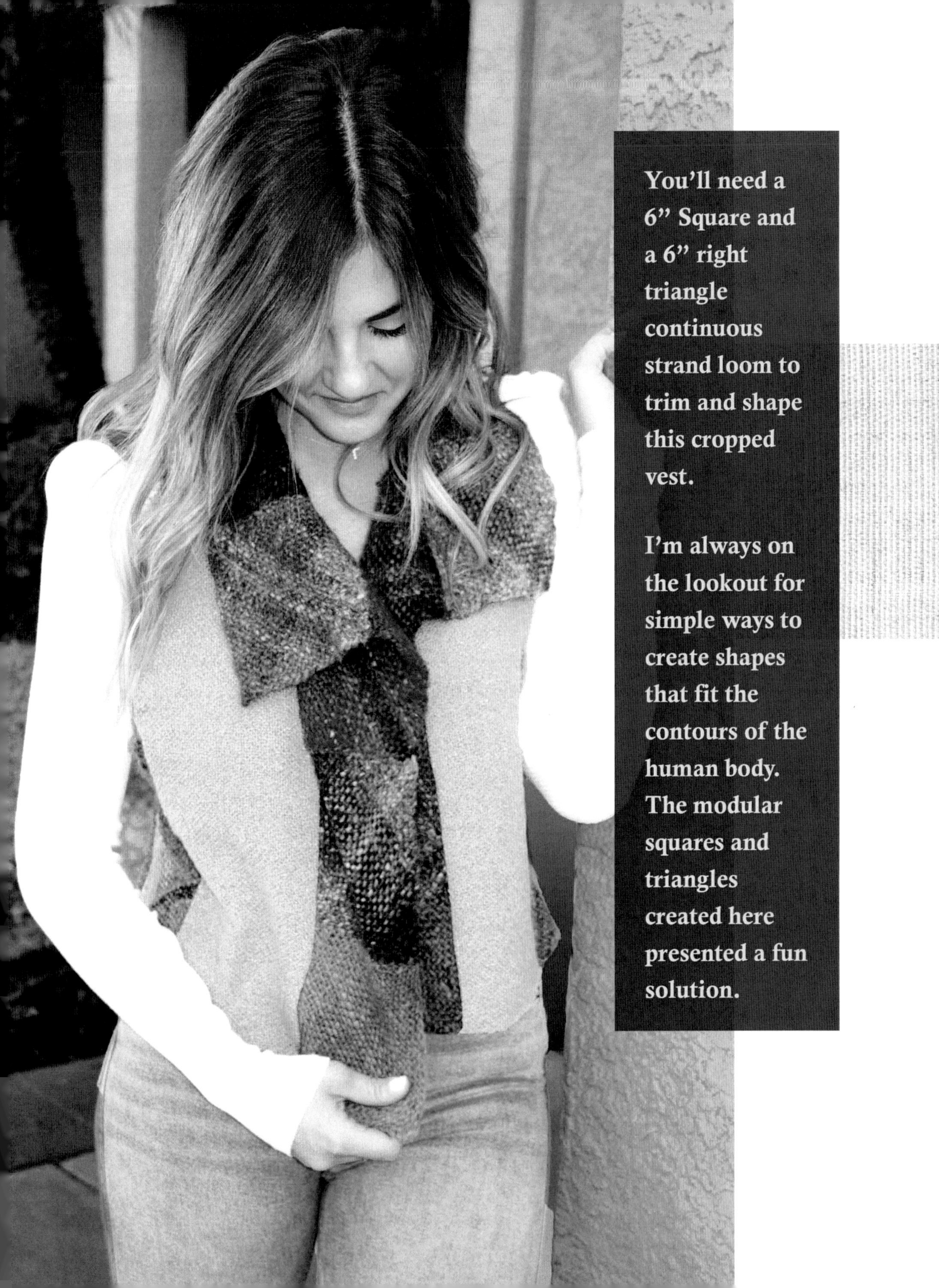
You'll need a 6" Square and a 6" right triangle continuous strand loom to trim and shape this cropped vest.

I'm always on the lookout for simple ways to create shapes that fit the contours of the human body. The modular squares and triangles created here presented a fun solution.

Patchwork Vest

This vest has a cropped length of about 20" from the shoulder for all sizes. Because it hangs open for a general fit, it is very accommodating for size. Wear the collar folded down, or flip it up and overlap for a sophisticated look.

I love the color opportunities and the textures provided by Noro's Ito yarn. However, if caught haphazardly in your crochet hook, it can break. If that happens to you, not to worry. I have an easy repair for that, p. 58.

A worsted or aran gauge yarn with some wool in it is your best bet for our squares and triangles as it will full in washing to increase the stability of the pieces.

	Small	Medium	Large
To fit bust sizes	32-34" (81.5-86.5 cm)	36-38" (91.5-96.5 cm)	40-42" (101.5-106.5)
Approx. width around high hip with overlap of the 5" squares in front	35" (89 cm)	39" (99 cm)	43" (109 cm)

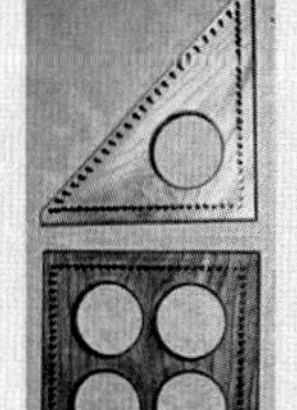

Equipment

- Loom that allows 10" (25.5 cm) weaving width
- 10 dent reed
- One shuttle
- 6" (15 cm) square and triangle continuous strand looms (I used the Mini-Mods set from Hillcreek Fiber Studio)
- For continuous strand weaving: size G/6 (4.00 mm).
- An inexpensive plastic hair pick works

  great as a weft beater for continuous strand looms.
- Sewing machine and coordinating thread

Body Panel Warp and Weft
3 balls of Berroco Quinoa in Millet, 91% cotton, 9% nylon, 50gm = 175 yd (159 m). Uses 415 yds (380.5 m) for the body panels warp and weft.

1 ball Noro Ito in color 19, 100% wool, 200 gm = 437 yds (400 m). Uses 197 yds (180 m). Use your left-over yarn for the pillow, p. 94.

All 3 sizes are prepared the same. The difference is in the width of the underarm inset.

Basic Weaving on the Continuous Strand Loom

You will need to make 6 triangles and 15 squares.

These looms usually come with instructions for the beginner. Regardless, here are the basics you will need to complete our simple one-color triangles and squares.

For many of us, a video is worth a thousand words when you are learning something new. You may want to check on youtube.com for instruction on this craft.

This looks trickier than it is. With either loom, you will feed the supply end of the yarn from above the upper edge of the loom. Think simply of pulling loops downward with the crochet hook, going under/over horizontal threads. The loops will then be spread open to place the right strand of the loop on a peg at the right and the left strand onto the corresponding peg at the left to create more horizontal threads. You will see that you get two weft picks for the effort of one with these looms.

Keep your tension relaxed but consistent, and pull the yarn from the center of the ball for easy flow.

Triangles - Setup (make 6)

I work with the loom flat on a table. With your 6" triangular loom long side (hypotenuse) on top as shown below, start with a slip knot (make a loop, then pull a loop of yarn through it). If you leave a tail of about 15" (38 cm) on two of the pieces, you will have yarn available to sew those triangles to the collar later.

Place the slip knot on peg #1 at the left. Draw the yarn across to the right under the top row of pegs and wrap it counter-clockwise around #2, then down around #3. Draw the yarn back to the left under #4, then up to the left of #5.

Weave

Breaks in the vertical red lines below represent yarn passing under the horizontal thread. No break shows it passing over a horizontal thread.

Start weaving at the left: Inserting the crochet hook over the bottom horizontal thread from your setup and under the top horizontal thread, pull a loop of the supply end of the yarn around the top of #5 down through those "warp" threads. Place the left side of the loop around #6. Draw the supply end of the yarn across to place the right side of that loop around #7 and up to the right of #8. I use my hook to pull the yarn in the direction of the arrows. The right side of that last loop will automatically have the same over/under that you see at the left. Use the hair pick or weft beater to straighten the weft lines at each side.

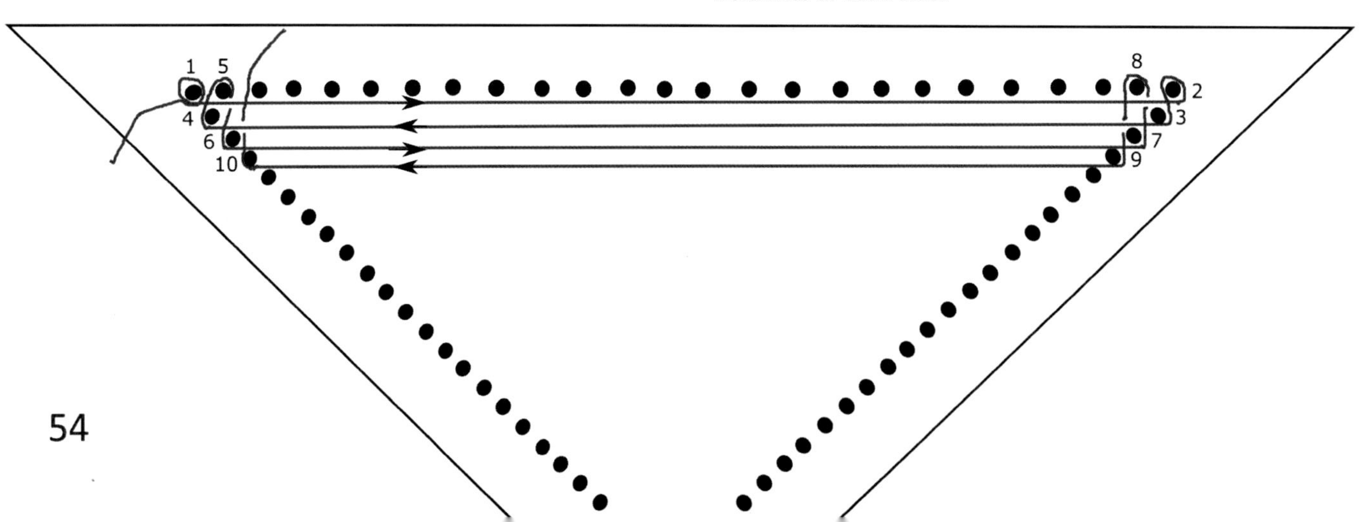

Some things to notice with triangles and squares:

- You will always be starting your hook over the bottom horizontal thread. Keeping that in mind will give you the right start every time.
- You will weave at both the right and left sides for triangles. For squares, you are weaving at the top right, and the left falls into place from there.
- Watch for errors where the yarn skips over or under more than one horizontal thread. You can fix these weft floats later, but it is easier to catch them while working. This usually shows up when you are weaving the next loop and notice that the pattern is disrupted. Make it a habit to check the previous loop as you weave and back up to fix any floats. If you catch that after removal, see fix #2 on p. 58.
- On the triangle, the loops over the top peg will straddle the first horizontal thread, meaning that the loop's left side will be an over strand, and the loop's right side will be under the top horizontal thread. If your loop doesn't do that, you didn't get the hook under the top warp thread when you drew that loop down. If you notice it early, back up and correct it. Otherwise, see #3 on p. 58.

Weave at the right side: now run the hook, bottom upward going over/under/over to pull the yarn down around #8 and onto #9. When you pull the working yarn across to place a loop onto #10, the same over/under/over will automatically be reflected. Repeat the left and right side movements until you have pulled the last loop at the center to place it on the bottom-most peg of the triangle.

Triangles - Finish

Your last loop must be separated with a single strand. Cut the working yarn long enough to extend through the middle of that center loop plus a tail for weaving in. Use the tapestry needle to weave between the 2 strands and weave in the tail.

You can pull the triangle off the pegs as is, but the long edge will be a little loose and "toothy" looking. This is good if you want to chain 2 triangles together to make a square, but we will be attaching this edge to a shorter square edge, so we will chain off the long edge to tighten it. This makes the edge curve a bit, which is perfect for our shaping.

Chaining Off the Long Edge

Before removing from the loom, use the crochet hook to pull the top right loop off peg #2. Working left across the top row of pegs, lift the 2nd loop off and pull it through the first one. Continue in this way, chaining across. When you are at the last loop at the top left, pull the hanging tail through the loop and tighten. Pull the rest of the triangle from the loom.

Squares - Setup (Make 15)

Pulling the yarn from the center of the ball, make a slip knot, but make sure the loop you pull up for this comes from the working end of the yarn and not from the tail end. This way, your slip knot will stretch to place it around peg #1 and #2, as highlighted below.

With the yarn ball above the top side of the frame, wrap the working yarn around #3, then over #4.

Weave

A break in the red line in the diagram below represents yarn passing under the horizontal threads. No break means it passes over.

The weaving is done from the upper right of the frame. The left side will fall into place from there.

Put the crochet hook over, then under the setup strands, and draw a loop around #4 downward. Place the right side of the loop around #5. With the crochet hook, draw the left side of that loop down to place it around #6. Continue up to place the supply end of the yarn around #7, then up around #8. Use your pick to beat the weft into straight lines at each side.

Repeat, alternating over/under/over at the right, then wrapping around the left pegs, and back to the right again until you get to the last loop on the bottom right peg. Use your weft pick to separate the final loop, cut a tail long enough to pass through the length of that loop, plus about 15" (38 cm), so you have a tail to use to sew squares together later. You will want to switch to the tapestry needle to bring this single tail through the last loop. Leave the tail hanging.

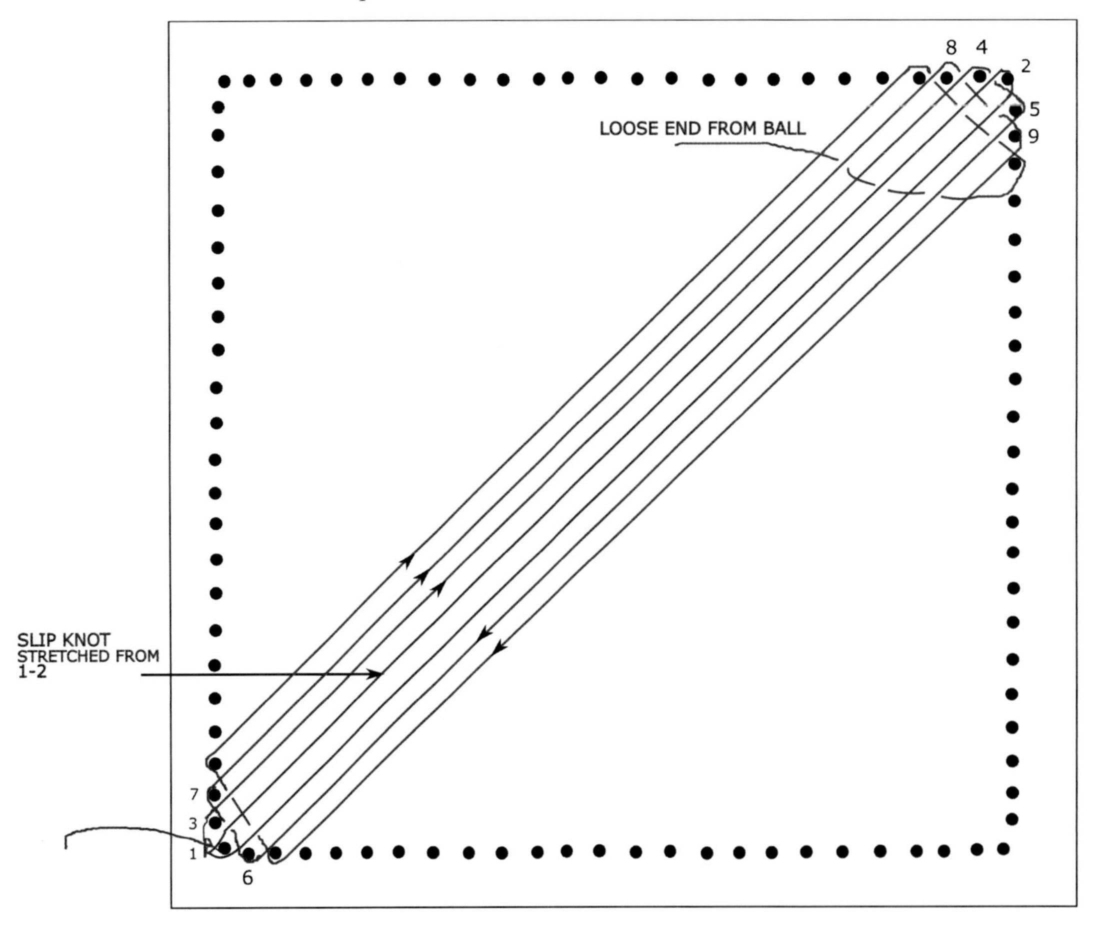

Squares - Finish

Pull the loops off the pegs. It helps to use the crochet hook to pull them off, working your way around a corner until you get the square loose enough to pull the piece off the loom gently. Don't get too aggressive here, or you might torque your square out of shape.

When all your squares and triangles are complete, wash according to method two on p. 12. Felting slightly will give your squares good shape and stability. Look at the pieces periodically as you rub them together in the wash water to determine the amount of fulling desired.

I wash these before stitching together as they tend to distort if strung together first.

Favorite Mistakes & Repairs for the Continuous Strand Loom

1 **I often skip a peg on the square loom** and don't discover it until I notice that I don't have the same number of pegs remaining at the side as I do at the top. It's a good idea to check periodically along all sides for this problem.

This repair is easy. As soon as you catch it, just use the crochet hook to lift loops from the peg and shift them over one-by-one.

2 **Skipping over or under** more than one horizontal thread (weft float). If you do this, both the right and the left strands will show a float. It is much better to unravel back to the error, but sometimes you don't notice this until the piece is off the loom. I recommend the following fix that I also use for repairing rigid heddle floats.

Thread your tapestry needle with a few inches of yarn. Start interweaving the supplemental yarn about two inches before the float, following the under/over pattern of the floating thread. Continue under/over along the float and for 1-2" (2.5 - 5 cm) beyond it. Cut the float in the middle. Once the piece has been washed and fulled, you can trim the hanging ends flush with the weaving.

3 **On the triangle, when a top loop doesn't surround the top horizontal thread:** You may find this as you are chaining along the long side of the triangle. You will see this error as a free loop in front of the horizontal thread. To keep the loop from unraveling, place it in back of the top horizontal thread, chain it, and continue.

4 **If your yarn breaks while weaving,** don't panic. Back the broken yarn end up to a peg, where you can have a tail long enough to tie it together with a new end in an overhand knot. You can weave the ends of this knot in after removing the piece from the loom. There will be a little knot there, but it will not be noticeable, especially if you include that edge into one of the seams later.

The panels woven on the rigid heddle will hang with a raw finished edge p. 18 (no hemming), so use a thread that is a good match. You will warp twice for this vest.

10 epi, 11 ppi

Front & Back Panels

We will refer to these later as the Quinoa front and Quinoa back panels to differentiate from the continuous strand weaving (referred to as the Ito pieces).

Warp for Front Panels

7" (18 cm) W x 63" (160 cm) L with Berroco Quinoa.

Weave Front Panels (make 2)

using Quinoa throughout for 20". Cut and tuck ending and beginning weft tails. Weave 2 picks of scrap yarn and weave a 2nd piece of the same length. Weave a footer, cut from the loom, and raw finish all ends.

Warp for Back Panel

10" (25.5 cm) W x 48" (122 cm) L with Quinoa.

Weave Back Panel

with Quinoa for 24" (61 cm).

Finish

Weave a footer, cut from the loom, and raw finish both ends. Wash according to method one, p. 12.

Assemble

Choose the color layout for the continuous strand squares and triangles: Lay out the squares and triangles as in Figure 1. If you can find a spot to leave your pieces laid out according to Diagram A, this will go together more efficiently. A shows the collar setup. Since the pieces will be multi-colored, think about balancing the lights and darks and colors.

The drawing below that (B) is for the underarm insets. You will use two triangles and two squares each for two of these. Here again, lay them out to decide how you want to balance those as well.

Notice that the triangles have the point cut off where they meet. This is because the underarm seam is adjusted to your size. Just overlap them for now as you lay them out to determine color arrangement. You will have two triangles left over for the shoulder shaping. We will label those 1 and 2.

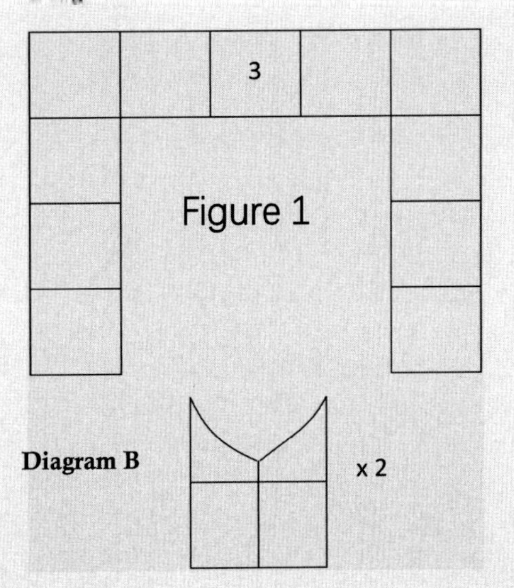

Attach the Quinoa Panels to the Ito pieces: Remove the top center square of your Figure 1 arrangement (labeled 3). Prepare the back Quinoa panel along one raw finished edge for gathering by sewing two rows close together within a 1/2" (1.5 cm) seam allowance using a long stitch (4mm) with no backstitching. Tie the threads on one side, gather the fabric evenly to match the bottom edge of square # 3, then tie the threads on the other end to hold the gather. With right sides together, adjust the gathered edge and sew the square to the back panel with a 5/8" (1.6 cm) allowance, Figure 2.

Now pin the 2 leftover triangles (1 and 2) to the Quinoa front panels. The curved edge is the hypotenuse (long edge) and should be facing upward as shown. Sew the bottom edge of these triangles to the front panels. Use a 1/4" (.5cm) seam allowance and make sure they finish as mirror images as shown. Press all seams downward after sewing.

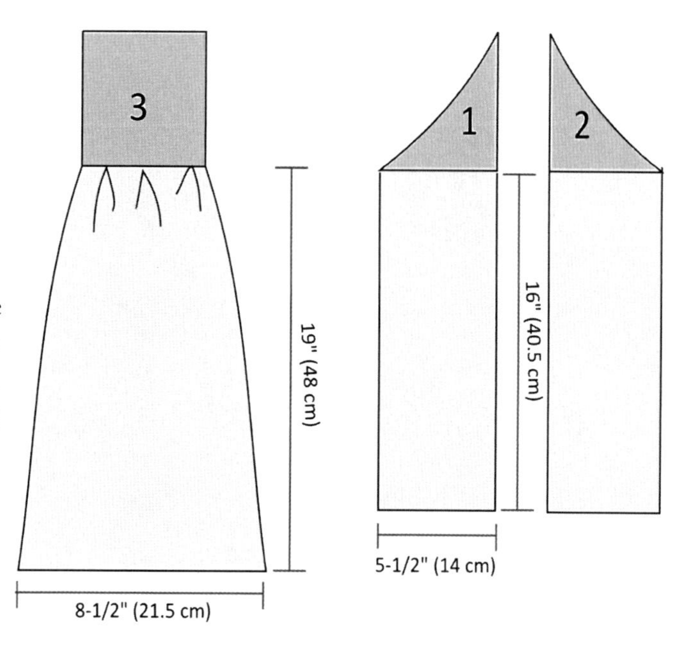

Figure 2

Stitch the rest of the squares together: You have 2 upside-down L shapes left in your layout. Hand stitch the 5 squares of each "L," end-to-end, in the order you have placed them.

I used a figure-eight stitch for a flat, barely visible seam (simulated at right). Line up the two edges to be sewn so the loops at the edge interlock like a puzzle (see right). Thread the tapestry needle with the square's hanging tail, or attach a strand of the Ito. From underneath, bring the needle up under the lowest edge loop then up under the first edge loop of the other piece. Continue in this fashion to the other edge. Weave in the hanging tails.

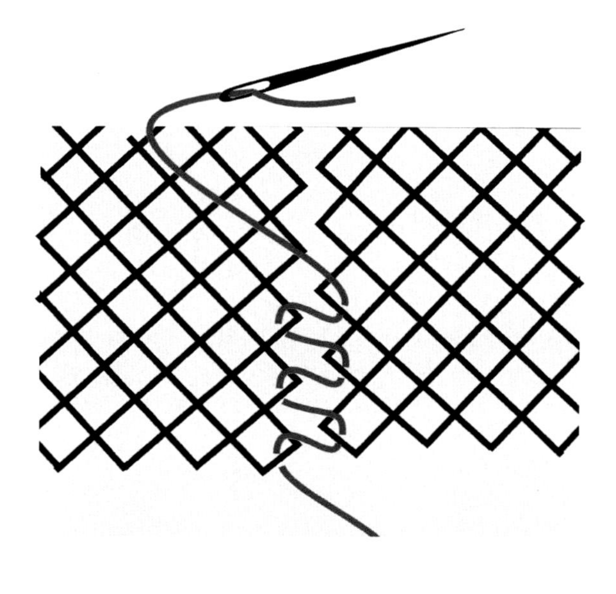

Figure 3

Attach the front panels to the collar: For placement, refer to figure 5 showing the right side of the finished vest. Use the same figure 8 stitch to attach the hypotenuse of each front panel you prepared to the square marked with *. You may have to ease these edges in to match.

Next, pin the front Quinoa panels to the inner edge of the front collar squares with right sides together. Sew with a 1/4" seam from the top down. It might be a little tight getting into the corner here to start. You can close any gap there by hand if needed. Your Quinoa panel may be slightly longer than the front collar edge. The woven pieces will hang with a raw edge, so if you need to even it up with the collar edge, double zigzag stitch again and trim if necessary. If the Quinoa panel is shorter, you can raw finish the square edge and trim it. Press the seam allowance away from the front.

Prepare the underarm insets: Hand stitch the four remaining triangles to their squares, as you laid out in Diagram B, Figure 1, with hypotenuse up using a figure 8 stitch. You will have four pieces that look like Figure 4 at left.

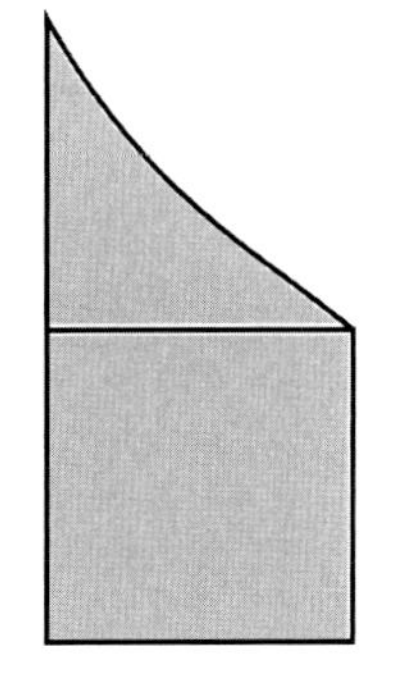

Figure 4

With right sides together, line up the long side of an inset piece to each Quinoa front panel from the bottom edge upward and sew with a 1/4" (.5 cm) seam allowance. Press the seam allowances toward the front. Attach the remaining two inset pieces to the back Quinoa panel in the same way, right sides together, and press these seam allowances toward the center back.

Underarm Seams: With right sides of the underarm insets together, sew a seam with an allowance of 2-1/4 (1-1/4, 1/4)", 5.5 (3, .5) cm. For the small and medium sizes, double zigzag this seam allowance together and trim it to 1/4" (.5cm). Press these seams toward the center back, and your vest is complete.

Figure 5

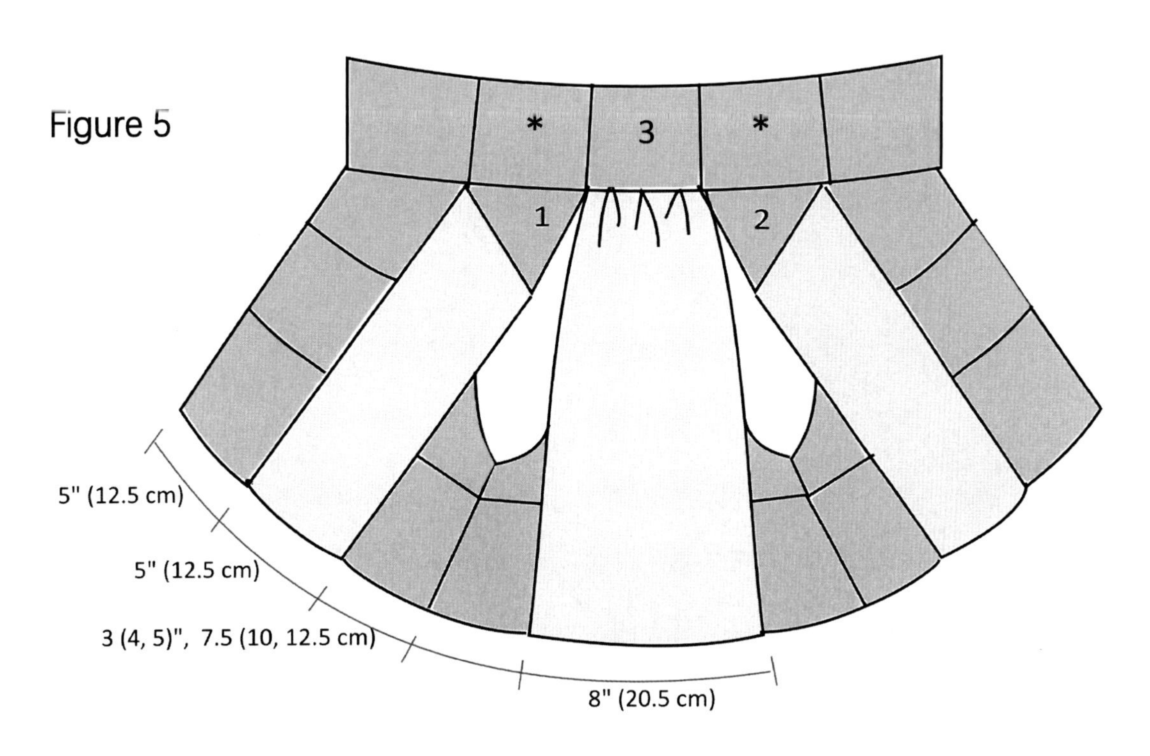

CARD
Mr. Harry

Chapter 3

> **"Creativity is allowing yourself to make mistakes. Art is knowing which ones to keep."**
>
> **- Scott Adams**

"You can't use up creativity. The more you use, the more you have. "

-Maya Angelou

Our creativity is like a muscle. If we exercise it, it will grow. If we fail to use it, it will atrophy. Human beings are seekers of comfort. We often crave our safe space, wrapping ourselves in the familiar to nurture our sense of security. There's nothing wrong with that essential urge. But to reach our full potential, we've got to leave that place. We need to locate that creative muscle and give it a good workout occasionally.

Remember that thrill of accomplishment you felt when you first learned your craft? If you're like many learners, you may have kicked out a series of scarves, maybe a placemat or two, or a couple of tea towels. Once you have enough rectangles, where do you look to regain that feeling of excitement? Maybe you're even one of those weavers who ran this course of early production, and now you've stashed that little loom in the closet, wondering why you invested in it in the first place. This chapter is intended to get you out of your shell, help you drag that rigid heddle from the closet, introduce an additional element to your weaving, and renew that sense of wonderment.

No more of that "I'm just not creative." excuse. If that is you, park those excuses at the door. I hope we make you just a little uncomfortable here to expand that inner and outer creative being that is you.

I have to admit it. This chapter's two inspired designs are probably the projects that pushed me from my comfort zone more than any others in this book. I decided to start with screen printing for the first piece, then added photo transfer to the second. Although I did a little silk screening on paper in my college days, it has been too many decades ago to have retained much.

Feeling a little reluctant to try something new as I was? This next artist is one of the most authoritative voices in breakout strategies for "getting your creative on" in the fiber arts practice. Whether you are out to make some art or just looking for inspiration to take the next step, "beyond the rectangle," grab your highlighter and let's go!

Jane Dunnewold

I was first introduced to Jane Dunnewold when I purchased her *Creative Strength Training,* an inspirational book aimed at seeking out and growing your creative skills.

A prolific fabric artist and educator with a career spanning nearly three decades, Jane has mounted multiple solo shows, been the recipient of a host of international awards, and authored numerous books on surface design and artistry in fabric. Her archives were recently acquired by the International Quilt Study Center and Museum in Lincoln, Nebraska.

I met Jane in San Antonio in her spacious and well-appointed studio where she works and conducts classes. She was enthusiastic about her online courses and master class offerings as well.

I found her to be an authentic and articulate voice to help others find their way through the maze of self-expression.

You can find out more about Jane at

www.janedunnewold.com.

Still Life With Cat

In your published words, you've mentioned overcoming difficult times in your life through your creative pursuits. If you could tell your younger self anything, what would it be?

If I had to point out anything to my younger self, it would be to spend some time thinking about what I wanted to do; not to just run on default or on all of the things that everybody else told me I should do. If I was giving somebody younger advice, and that's what I do, I'd ask two questions: "Ok, what's practical, and what do you want to do?" It goes by so fast. If you can possibly manage it, it's good to be doing what you want to do. It's what I think of as alignment. Alignment is when what you love to do and what you are good at doing are somehow tag-teaming.

The other thing I would say is, "Take a deep breath and roll with it because it is going to work out one way or another." This doesn't mean that what happens is always what you want to happen, but it means that you're going to be capable of whatever it is.

You use a lot of symbology in your work. Would you describe your process, your choices, as more intuitive or more intellectual?

I think it's a mix. In my situation, I've had a life where I had to totally figure it out on my own. I had to develop my practical side. That side looks at something and strips it down to what it really needs to be. I think that's good. But the intuitive side always begins the process. I didn't realize that until I had been working as an artist for a while - all of the series I've created started with some lightbulb moment. Lots of times, these come at 4:00 in the morning, or I may wake up with an idea.

One time I was looking out the window of my office where my studio was and saw these pigeons landing on a wire. Every time a new pigeon landed, they all scooched over, so they were the same distance apart. I thought, "Isn't that interesting. They have healthier boundaries than humans do." That intuitive realization spawned a series of 15 pieces about boundaries and human beings and how we allow borders to control us in ways that are frequently negative. Animals migrate wherever they have to go. They don't give a damn whether it's the US or Mexico.

So the intuitive hit is usually there, and it sparks the initial idea. After that, I go about things rather deliberately. I put down words at the top of a page, then use free association to connect the dots out of my unconscious onto the paper. That's where the symbols come from, so what represents boundaries: maps, birds on wires, wholesnesses, the moon, the sun, roundness. I explore all of that, and it guides me to make the tools I create.

These tools are basically for printing because I'm a surface designer by nature. Then, when I've got

Etude #23

those all ready to go, they fit together seamlessly because I did thc work. After that, it goes back to intuitive playtime.

What kind of planning and research do you do before beginning your work?

I'm big on series. One thing we tease apart in my advanced classes is what's going on with something that isn't working. Sometimes it's because there are two pieces slammed into each other instead of being two separate pieces.

Once you learn to use free association and the strategies I use to come up with designs, tools, etc., you realize that if it's got a lot of juice to it, it is going to take a series of pieces.

If I work in a series, I'm thinking long term about what is going into it. I also, at that point, think about limiting what the variables are. I was invited to do a show where I realized I was going to need 40 pieces. How was I going to get 40 pieces done in 8 months? So I thought, "Ok, I'm going to need to limit the variables, so I don't have so many choices to make." I had to decide in advance that each piece was going to be between 12-18" tall and 20-35" wide, so they would all fit together in the space. I'm going to work only in grey, white and black to see how far I can carry that. I'm going to start each week by dyeing four pieces of fabric in that rough size. So done, boom, decided. It sounds very regimented, but it's actually a system within which there is a lot of freedom.

If it's something more topical, I shouldn't admit it, but I love Google. If you're curious, it's so useful because it's so much more instantaneous than flipping through a dictionary or encyclopedia. I was thinking about the fact that I always use the word strategies. I've been very deliberate in what I write, choosing my words so they have meat to

Zebra Thistle

them, and I can turn them into my own language. So I looked up strategies, and it means layers, strata. It's layers of the work that you do; it's layers of who you are as a human being. A strategist is the master of the layers. We are the master or mistress of our layers, whether it's choosing our colors, or warping the loom, or adding the embellishments, or whatever it is. It made it so much more profound by understanding what the word meant in a way that I had never thought about before.

In your book, *Creative Strength Training*, you offer several ideas for overcoming stumbling blocks. What are some of your favorite strategies to become unblocked?

I used to have a studio on the 3rd floor of a dilapidated church building. What I loved about it was that everything around it was in disrepair also.

Sometimes when I had a student who was stuck, I would get some oranges from the store and make the student stand at the 3rd-floor window and throw oranges onto the parking lot across the street to see them splat!

Another exercise I did was tape a paper tablecloth down on the sidewalk below and had people pour paint on it from the window.

A big thing to do when you don't have the advantage of a 3rd-floor window is tape a large piece of paper to the floor, then take some cheap black paint and a broom and draw with the broom in really big brushstrokes. We get so tight, which is part of being stuck. Students will usually do these exercises, and they immediately break the block.

I don't get a chance to do these as much as I used to, although I've done them, and I know how they feel. My version of it now is, like with the piece I was working on last week. I had gone as far as putting this very large focal point on it and fusing it down, so it's done, Jane!

I kept looking at it and thinking, "It's not right." The proportions just weren't right. Finally, I just ripped it off. There were all the little tears in it. I was going to have to deal with it. Fortunately, I was able to cover the damage that was there and reestablish the focal point. For me, I have to be stuck long enough that I will do just about anything to get out of it. It's like when you're standing on the edge of a swimming pool, knowing it's going to be really cold and you have to jump in. Finally, you dive in, and it's great and refreshing. That period of angst almost has to be there. You have to get so fed up that the tide turns, and you're just going to do it.

What advice would you offer to those among us who may suffer from a feeling of inadequacy in their work?

I'm very interested in archetypes and how those symbolic patterns address human behavior.

There's an archetype called the wounded healer. This is the person who can heal other people because she herself has experienced whatever the student is going through. I don't have a degree in art: I'm completely self-taught. I was going to go into the ministry.

I have a degree in psychology. That has been really useful, partly for the teaching that I do and partly because that's what has introduced me to all these wonderful symbolic references that come back into my work.

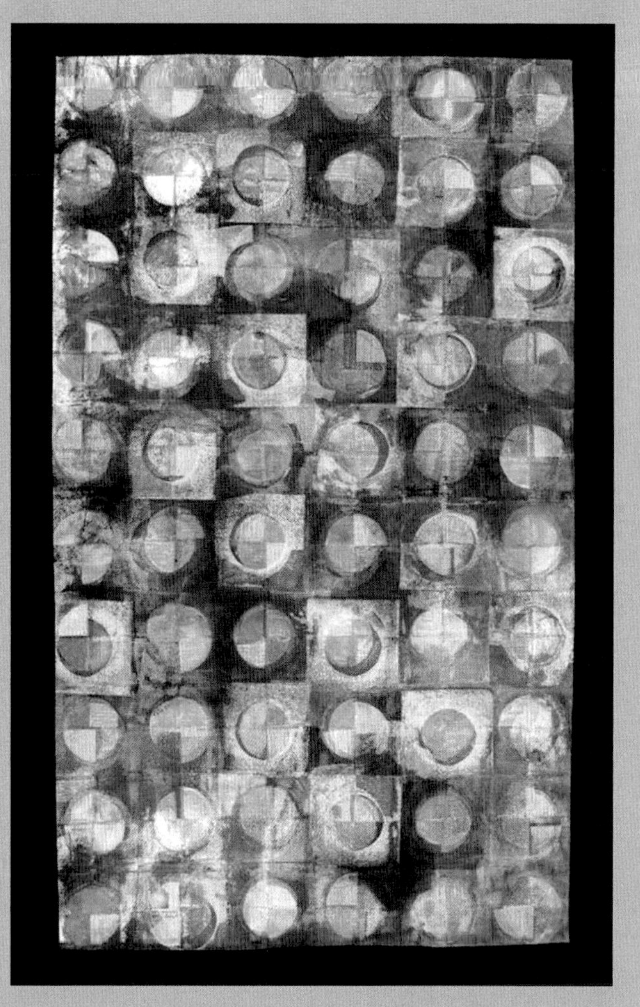

Structure #1: Messengers

I've worked very hard to be a good teacher, and part of that is recognizing when students feel as though they are not good enough. So I call it out. The first thing I say in the morning of our first class is, "We're not going to look around and say, "Oh, hers is better, or HERS is better, and what am I doing here. Let's acknowledge that's what we all do, so we can put all that negative energy outside the door, come back in here, close the door; this is our sacred space for creating."

What currently influences you, and where do you see that going in your future work?

It's important for me to continue the teaching that I do. I don't teach surface design as much as I teach self-actualization as an artist. The master program that I run is a 2-1/2 year program where the same people come back five times. I'm shifting from technique and process to interior development. I see the next few years of my career focusing on that because it kind of comes full circle to my psychology background.

From an artistic standpoint, I've consciously decided that I want to work smaller. I spent a lot of the early parts of my career working bigger. I see my work as scaling down in size. Part of this is to make my work more accessible to people who would like to have a piece but can't afford it or doesn't have the room for it.

Also, I'm much more interested in working with pre-existing vintage materials rather than creating brand new cloth from white fabric. With so much stuff in the world now, I've gotten more involved in appropriating vintage embroidery made by some unknown maker that has now shown up at Goodwill. I'm also interested in unfinished quilt blocks, or things that can be used to complete a story that somebody else started.

What are a couple of parting thoughts you might provide to encourage our readers to find inspiration?

I think it's a good idea, because we all have phones and cameras, to pick a topic each month. You can make a list of a year's worth of ideas in advance if you like. I'm taking this from an exercise in a class we do online called "The Creative Eye." I pick a topic each month like "sky," and everyone is challenged to post pictures that represent the sky on this private forum page. So there are pictures of the sky reflected in windows and sunsets, of course. Every single day there is a new way to see the sky, so spend that month with the camera taking pictures that represent your topic. The crazy thing about noticing is that it's everywhere as soon as something comes onto your radar. It's a great way of establishing a habit of really looking at what is around you.

Another thing is to surf around on YouTube and look at things other people are doing. Sometimes I type words randomly, like "Funny Art," because I have to research the videos that I create. Don't remain the observer. If it looks fun, don't just think, "Oh, I would never do that." Do it! Buy the little pens that they've got there or whatever it is. Order it and set aside a day to explore it. That's why classes are good. A teacher makes you do things that you will not do yourself.

Frieda's Gate

Nobody will make a coal garden [i.e., a colorful spiked creation made from coal and simple materials] unless a teacher makes them do it. Pretty soon, you're open to all kinds of things you wouldn't have tried. That stretches the creativity and builds the muscle memory.

Surface design on fabric is a broad and beautiful study. I narrowed it down to a little printing and photo transfer in the two pieces in this chapter.

This will allow you to dip your toe in the water without making a big investment upfront.

Folium and Sphere Cowl

This cowl (or optional scarf length) is done with a clasped warp to create the vertical color changes shown. Instructions for this special warp are in the pattern that follows. You may choose to repurpose a previously woven piece that just needs a little extra jazz instead.

If you weave the clasped warp pattern, you can adjust the number of color changes depending on the available yardage you have. This one is great for using up small quantities from your yarn stash.

Finished Measurements approx. 9-1/2" (24 cm) W x 41" (104 cm) L for cowl length. 70" (178 cm) L for scarf - changes in parenthesis.

Equipment for Weaving

- Rigid heddle loom with at least 12" (30.5 cm) weaving width
- 8 dent reed
- 1 stick shuttle

Warp: You will want to use plant-derived fibers such as bamboo, Tencel, rayon, or organic cotton yarn for good printing results in a DK (3/2) or sport gauge. Don't use synthetic or protein fibers such as wool as they won't accept the dye effectively. I used Interlacements ZigZag, 100% rayon, 8 oz. = 500 yds (457 m).

Color 1: Olive uses 178 (260) yds, 160 (235) m
Color 2: Brown uses 125 (182) yds, 111.5 (163.5) m
Color 3: Champagne uses 43 (62) yds, 36.5 (54)m

Weft: Fingering gauge (5/2) bamboo, Tencel, or rayon. Uses 137 (235) yds, 125.5 (215) m. I used Dragon Tale 5/2 rayon in Olive, 8 oz. = 1050 yds (960 m).

For Printing:

- Household rubber gloves or disposable nitrile gloves (optional)
- Small squeegee or old plastic credit card, key card, or loyalty card to use as a squeegee
- Fabric paint - avoid glitter paint as this may clog your screen.
- Thermofax screens with designs of your choice
- Worktable and scrap fabric (I used muslin) to allow 4 layers to cushion the work and absorb paint
- Scrap cardboard to fit under your printing area and T pins to secure the fabric to the cardboard
- I was very messy and glad that I had a cheap, paper table cloth to cover my work area.

Creating a Clasped Warp

Sett: 16 epi, 9-10 dpi

Getting the placement of your clasped warp right requires a little practice to get the adjustments in the right place as you go. This pattern calls out several color changes, but it will still be beautiful if you wish to work across the warp in the same two-color scheme or create your own combination of color changes.

With the rayon content and minimal take up of the lweft, there will be very little contraction in the woven length.

Warp

11-3/4" (30 cm) W x 66" (167.5 cm) L for cowl or 96" (244 cm) L to weave a scarf of approximately 70"(178 cm) finished length = 94 ends where a double-strand counts as one.

With the back of the loom facing you, plan to draw loops through every hole and every slot. This will double the warp strand and make a close sett so that the warp is dominant. To improve the drape and emphasize the vertical pattern, I recommend a lightweight weft when the sett is this close.

The magic is all in the warp on this one. Once the loom is warped, the rest is simple, one-color plain weave.

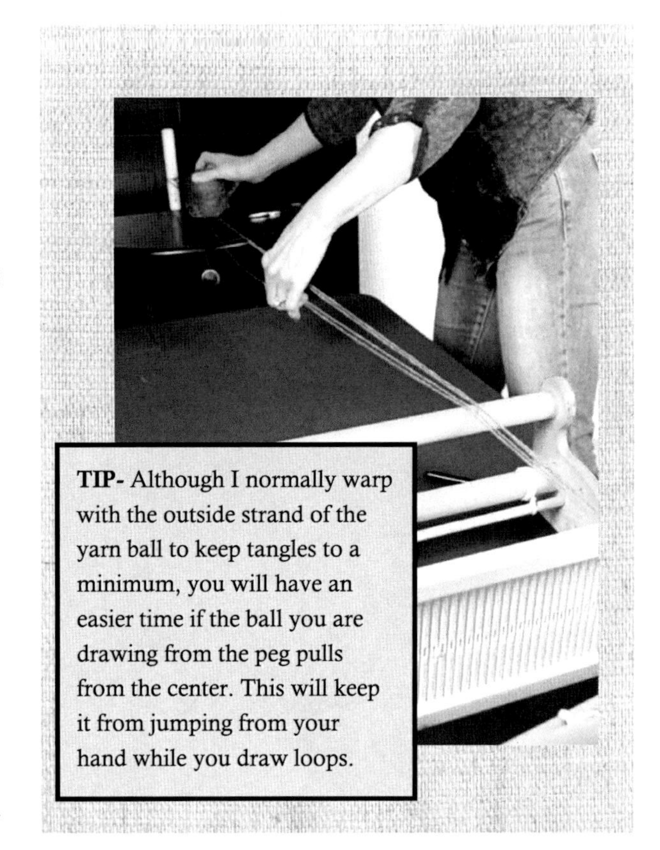

TIP- Although I normally warp with the outside strand of the yarn ball to keep tangles to a minimum, you will have an easier time if the ball you are drawing from the peg pulls from the center. This will keep it from jumping from your hand while you draw loops.

1 With Color 1 tied at the back apron rod and with Color 2 tied to the warping peg, sley your first loop of Color 1 through the slot at the starting edge of the loom. Bring that loop forward through the reed, stopping about 2/3 of the distance to the peg. Pick up the ball that you tied to the peg and bring it toward the loop just drawn, passing this ball through the loop and back around the peg. Now you have your first clasp.

You can tighten up the slack and adjust the clasp location by pulling gently on the balls of yarn at

Figure 1

either end. The goal is to keep the point where the warp threads clasp at the desired location. A little slack in the warp here and there is fine.

To clarify color changes: to remove a color will be to "tie off." Adding a color will be to "tie on."

2 Your next loop will have Color 1 drawn through the neighboring hole. **Continue drawing through slots, then holes, completing a total of 20 clasps arranged around that first location. Some will be closer to the loom, some farther, to make the transition interesting, as shown in Figures 1 and 2.

3 Continuing with Color 1 at the apron rod, cut Color 2 and tie off at the peg. Tie Color 3 onto the peg and complete 5 clasps.

4 Cut Color 3 and tie off to the peg. Tie Color 2 onto the peg. Repeat the color changes from ** in step 2 through step 3 once more.

5 Cut and tie off Color 3 to the peg. Tie on Color 2 at the peg, and create 20 more clasps.

6 For the **directional color shift** (seen below), cut and tie off Color 1 to the apron rod. Cut and tie off Color 2 to the peg, tie Color 2 onto the rod, and Color 1 onto the peg. Complete 5 clasps arranging them around the same focal area established at the beginning.

7 Cut and tie off Color 1 to the peg leaving Color 2 in place at the loom apron rod. Tie Color 3 onto the peg and finish with 20 clasps of this combination.

8 Cut and tie off Color 2 to the apron rod and Color 1 to the peg.

9 Now cut the loops at the peg, cutting through the loops created where tied there. The extra yarn from these ties will slide off the cut ends.

10 Tie all ends together in a loose knot, wind the warp onto the back beam, and tie onto the front apron rod in 1" bundles as usual - no need to sley the reed. You will have 2 ends in every slot and hole.

Weave

Plain weave with fingering gauge (5/2) rayon for 42" (107 cm), or 72" (183 cm) if warped for the scarf.

Finish

Cut and tuck the ending tail, and remove from the loom, tying 4 strand tassels at both ends.

Wash according to method one, p. 12. When dry, trim the fringe to the desired length and trim any hanging tails flush.

Figure 2

Screen Printing

The fabric paint will lend some stiffness to the fabric where applied, but the rayon will assure maximum overall drape of the printed piece. Our woven pieces tend to have texture that may prevent the screened image from being as crisp as a smooth commercially woven fabric, but you will still achieve some wonderful decorative results.

I acquired the 2 screens at right from www.janedunnewold.com. Your choices (including ordering custom designs) are endless. Note that the squeegee side is clearly labeled. This side is the textured side. If you make sure it faces upward when printing, your screen will last longer.

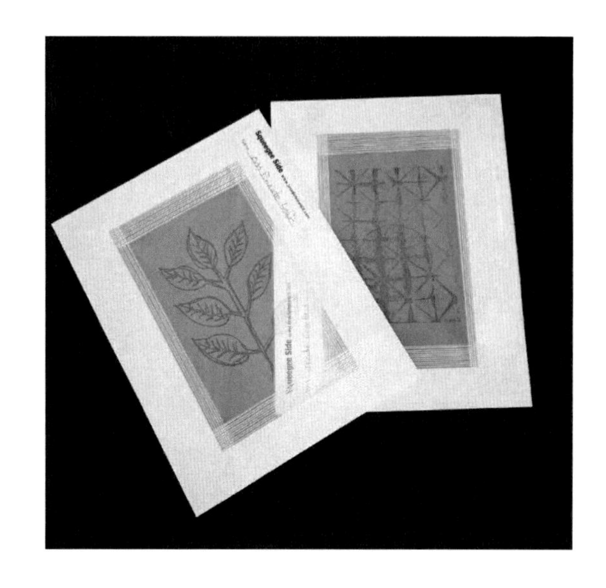

Preparing Your Work Surface

Since I don't have a padded table to pin my fabric down, I covered my folding table with a paper table cloth, placed a piece of cardboard on that, and covered it with four layers of scrap muslin to absorb the paint. Smooth out the surface so that no wrinkles are there to interfere with your printing. My workspace was big enough to accommodate one screen at a time.

Important - Make sure you test on scrap weaving before proceeding!

Instructions

1 Pin the fabric to the padded surface you created. This will keep it from lifting when you remove the screen.

2 Place the screen where you want to print. You may want to wear protective gloves to keep from having to scrub paint from your fingernails after working.

3 I chose an old plastic loyalty card as a squeegee. You can use this or a spoon to lay some fabric paint along the top of the screen frame above the image (about 2 tablespoons worth).

4 Holding the screen with one hand, use the other hand to hold the plastic card and pull the paint towards you across the image as perpendicular to the screen as possible.

You will be able to see if you did not pull enough paint all the way down to complete the image. Scoop up excess paint or apply more as needed and squeegee top-down again if required. Otherwise, I found fewer passes result in a sharper image as long as you have forced enough paint through the screen to complete the design.

5 Pick up the screen and remove it carefully from the fabric.

Repeat the process for additional printing as desired with caution. If you are repeating an image, not overlapping, you can proceed without waiting for the paint to dry, BUT be careful to place a clean piece of paper (without shifting it) over what you just printed to cover anywhere that the screen front could touch the wet paint. It is easy to smear paint from your hands or that clings to your screen frame onto the fabric. Once it gets on the fabric, it is permanent, so work cleanly and carefully. I'll repeat, PRACTICE, PRACTICE, PRACTICE.

Your first images must dry for at least 24 hours before overprinting on them.

Work quickly with each printing session as the fabric paint dries fast. You will need to wash your screen with warm water, mild soap, and a soft brush or sponge to remove all paint from the mesh and corners of the screen before it dries and clogs the image.

The frame and screen will stain with color, but you only need to be concerned with making sure the opaque areas of paint are removed from the screen's print area. Hold it up to the light to make sure it is clear, and dry the screen completely before the next printing session. Water droplets on the screen can affect your printing.

Let your piece dry for 3-4 days if you will be washing it.

I can't leave the subject of surface design without creating a little art piece for the wall.

Here we'll add a focal point in the form of a photo transfer to make this decorative wall hanging.

Folium and Fairies Wall Hanging

To introduce a third element for this piece, I tried Jane's suggestion. I started writing words down that would associate with the natural forms I had chosen for the screen printing: nature, plants, floral, wings, feminine, fairies. With those ideas in mind, I found the line drawing, shown at right, on the internet. This image is considered public domain, not subject to copyright laws.

You may have your own photo, or there are several websites where you can obtain royalty-free, no accreditation (no credit to the photographer required) in the resources section. On both moral and legal grounds, It is important to respect the rights that are due to the originator of any words or images we appropriate.

Finished Measurements approximately 11" (28 cm) W x 19" (49 cm) L

Equipment and Materials

- Laser copy of the image you want to transfer - I went to the local office supply store to make mine.
- Woven scrap for the foundation. I salvaged one side of a linen cowl that wasn't being worn. Be sure to select natural plant based fiber to accept the paint effectively.
- A small piece of light colored or light neutral fabric (plant based fiber) for photo transfer
- Sewing machine and thread or needle and thread to secure fabric piece to the weaving
- Household rubber gloves or disposable nitrile gloves
- Expired plastic credit card, key card, or loyalty card to use as a squeegee (or a small squeegee)
- Kitchen spoon for burnishing the transfer
- Citrasolv cleaner and glass (not plastic) bowl or jar to hold a small quantity
- Sponge or sponge brush to apply Citrasolv. I cut a piece of memory foam I had on hand.
- Fabric paint, non-glitter
- Masking tape
- Thermofax screens with designs of your choice
- Work table and scrap fabric (I used muslin) to allow 4 layers to cushion the work and absorb paint
- Scrap cardboard to fit under your printing area and T pins to secure the fabric to the cardboard
- Cheap plastic table cloth to cover the work area
- Colored or soft graphite pencils to sharpen transfer image (optional)
- Hanging Poster frame (optional)

Instructions

Test your transfer technique on scrap cloth first.

I completed this photo transfer with the Citrasolv, a plant based solvent commonly used as a household cleaner. Although less toxic than other solvents for this purpose, it is highly concentrated and can be irritating to the skin, so protective gloves are advised. You can find several videos for this process at www.citrasolv.com/image-transfers-1.

1 **Prepare the woven foundation:** You will need a rectangle of woven fabric big enough to hold the transfer piece and to do a little screen printing at the top and bottom plus approximately 1" (2.5 cm) at each end to fold into the frame if you choose. You can weave something new or upcycle something old for this. I used the V cowl shown at top right. Although I liked the fabric, it just didn't have much drape, so it was never worn. I had knitted around the perimeter and crocheted around the interior of the cowl when it was made and wanted to incorporate this in the new piece. I raw finished edges with my sewing machine before cutting apart as needed to get a rectangle 10-1/2" (26.5 cm) x 21" (53.5 cm).

2 **If you are screen printing the edges of the rectangle** like I did, do this now according to the instructions on p. 74-75.

For the transfer piece, you will need a copy from a toner-based printer. Your inkjet printer at home will not work for this process. I ran to the office supply store and had 3 copies printed for both the color and black and white photos on the next page. Since a copy is only good for one use, I wanted extra for practice. You can often email the photos to the

store from home or take your laptop or phone with you to do this on site.

Note that your transfer will reverse the resulting image, so you may want to flip your photo before printing if that is a concern, particularly if you transfer words or numbers! Reversing a photo can be done in several ways, depending on the operating system you use. One simple method for any computer is to go to a free online photo editor like Pixer.us. Click "Choose File" at the top left to get the photo from your computer, then "Upload & Edit." Be patient. The editor may be slow. On the next line of commands, select "Flip," then "Horizontal," and save it to your computer.

3 **Prepare the fabric for the transfer**. I used commercially made fabric to apply to my woven background. Transfers are subtle and transparent, and my handwoven fabric would be too textural for the best effect. Again, you need to choose a natural, plant-derived cloth. I chose a lightly textured cotton/linen blend because it matched my weaving nicely. I might have gotten a sharper image with something smoother, but I am satisfied with this choice.

Silk is one of the best options for the clearest transfer if that matters to you.

I unraveled the top few strands of the fabric to help align my image to the grain. Use the same work surface setup as for the screen printing, and tape or pin this fabric to the work surface.

4 **Prepare the transfer:** Place your fabric right side up and the image ink side down. Tape the transfer page to the fabric.

5 **Apply the Citrasolv** to the back of the transfer page with a foam sponge or a brush. Wet the paper, but don't overdo it.

6 **Burnish it:** Using the back of a spoon and holding the image as extra protection against shifting, burnish the image firmly and completely. You can lift one corner just slightly to check your work, but be careful not to reposition the copy.

My first effort was a little blurry. I had burnished too aggressively and let the fabric slip, so I tried again. Consistently, the results were clearer from the color copy than the black and white even though I had a fairly dark image - see the photos at left. I expected the black and white to transfer more readily. My results might have been relevant to the printer used, which is why it pays to experiment. Different printers may yield different effects.

7 **I touched up my transfer** with a little application of colored pencil to sharpen some of the lines. A soft graphite pencil will also work. I also unraveled a few strands around all sides of my fabric for a rustic effect.

8 **Attach the transfer to the woven foundation:** Place this piece on top of your woven/printed foundation, pin it to the weaving, and stitch the transfer piece in place. I used a zigzag stretch stitch around the edges with my simple machine, as this is a double stitch that shows up well.

9 **Hang it:** I found an inexpensive 13" poster hanger online that was an easy way to turn this into a wall hanging, shown assembled on p. 62.

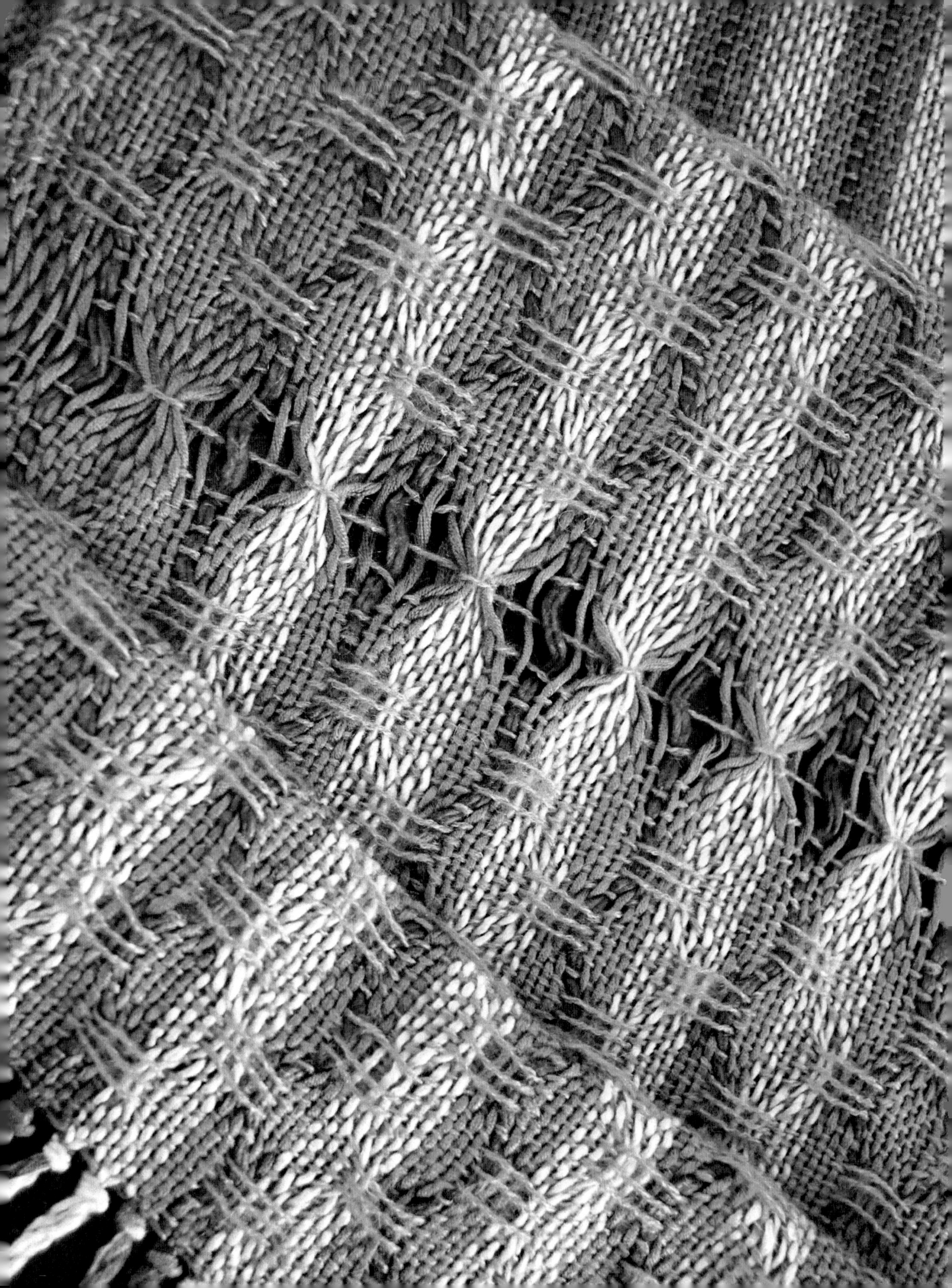

Chapter 4

> **"When you do things for their own sake, that's when you create your best work. That's when it's art."**
>
> **-Naval Ravikant**

"Tell your own story, and you will be interesting. "

Louise Bourgeois

As a painter, and later as a weave-it-to-wear-it designer, It took me many years to realize that finding the direction for what we create should be more about figuring out what we want our creative life to be about than trying to produce just what others think we should.

Of course, we fret over things like color choices, fit, style, composing the elements, etc., so that our audience will be pleased. However, to make our work come together in the most meaningful way, we should first understand what has inspired us and consider this foremost as we direct our efforts.

This process doesn't have to be complicated or even too deep. Not everyone is planning to set the world on fire with originality. I'm suggesting here that our fiber experience, whether artist or happy maker, might be a richer one if we consider some goals before we embark upon our craft.

For example, I planned early in my weaving career, a fan of natural fibers and fashion that I am, to create (mostly) wearables from quality fibers that feel great and achieve an element of drape and shape. I wanted a more urban or contemporary appeal than I was finding in the rigid heddle world at that time. I have worked under those principles to exceed traditional expectations of rigid heddle weaving.

One particular moment in my life helped to shape my interest in garment making from the rigid heddle. When I was 10 years old, a friend's grandmother took sheets of newspaper and sewed us some fun pleated skirts and other simple outfits. I still remember my awe at the range of possibilities to be had from the simplest materials.

Additionally, I am that middle child pursuing peace and harmony, so most of my color choices lean toward the subdued or harmonious rather than glitzy or bold selections. Perhaps you are one who loves vivid, bright color? Do you prefer using your skills to decorate your nest, or conversely, are you someone who might use their weaving for dramatic artworks? You go, girl or guy!

By figuring yourself out in this way and venturing forth with confidence, you will have less confusion and more positive results from your craft.

My next artist has achieved world recognition by deciding exactly who she is and what she wants from her work. She describes reaching a place where validation has come from embracing her own thinking style and not succumbing to the outside pressures.

After reading her story, take a moment to jot down some thoughts on who you are and how this can affect your choices when you weave. Compare these ideas to the work you have done so far. Are you on track? If so, were your choices conscious or subconscious? If not, how might this change your decisions going forward?

Cornelia Tuttle Hamilton

Cornelia and I worked together on a project for a major yarn company several years ago. We hit it off right away, amidst all the chaos and life changes we both shared at that time. Since then, we try to reconnect whenever I get through Atlanta to share a coffee or a martini or two!

With her inquisitive spirit and zest for life, Cornelia is a prolific creator of original designs for the knitter. Her work has been featured extensively in American as well as European publications such as Vogue Knitting, Creative Knitting, Knitting (Danmark), Allers, Dröm Hem & Trädgård, Allas, Svensk Damtidning. She has also authored 15 knitting books and ebooks and has been hosted by multiple bloggers and online interviewers seeking to unlock some of her creative secrets.

Splitting her time between the lifestyle she loves in Atlanta and her yarn shop in Mariefred, Sweden, where she spends time with her sons, Cornelia can be known as a straightforward, no pretense type person with a passion for yarn (especially Noro, for whom she wrote much of her work).

See more of Cornelia's designs and signature yarn line at www.hamiltonyarns.com.

Your designs show a strong sense of structure as well as surface texture. What is the thought process you go through to convey this message?

The things that inspire me are nature, architecture, light and shadow, and a strong diagonal. I like stitch patterns that have a strong diagonal because knitting is very geometrical. I do a little bit of asymmetrical work, but not much. The asymmetrical stuff is really just about the geometry.

When I was younger, I was a little bit frustrated because I realized that my work might have been too ordinary; that it lacked "quirkiness," Then I realized that my brain is pretty balanced, and that is reflected in my design. I like balance.

There are what I call surface designers who select a yarn and a design and then apply a stitch to it. That can be done on paper because it's two dimensional. When I design, it's already a multi-dimensional thing. This has allowed me to apply the negative and positive space, the light and dark. It's like sculpture, which is what I want to do with my art.

Do you do a lot of advance planning, or do you work more intuitively?

Well, I've had to keep an eye on interpreting what is coming next in terms of wearable fashion and color, and there is some connection between fashion and interior design color that I follow. In fashion, being too early is as bad as being too late. The knit world follows fashion rather than creating it, and I've had to be aware of that.

As far as planning, I'm not very scientific. I'm very spontaneous instead. I follow whims as they come. That can be at 10:00 at night or 3:00 in the morning. I don't see any difference between my life and my work. That's not necessarily good, but that's me. I just try to stay open to those moments and use them as they come.

You have a prolific body of work. What keeps you going?

What I don't want to do is repeat myself. What I've tried to do is keep myself entertained. I need to be stimulated intellectually by doing something different and new.

Then I just keep moving forward and developing. It's about solving problems. I take things as they come up, and then I solve problems.

It used to bother me that you had to deal with so many constraints before you could get a design out. It's not like standing in front of a canvas and just being able to put down anything you want. I've learned to appreciate being good at making a lot out of these constraints.

I've always strived to make something that looks complicated but is easy to execute. I look at my stuff as a jumping-off point. The happiest I get is when I see someone take a basic design that I've done and change it. I like to help people move past just following what someone else has done.

The last time we talked about it, you were expressing a fascination with holes in your work. What is your current direction?

I have a piece in Vogue Knitting right now that I just posted online. It's combining a chevron with my drop stitch openwork, so the holes are continuing.

I think of knitting itself as a craft, but I'm interested in knitting as an art medium as well, as my paintbrush, so to speak. I would like to move into something that is more art where I don't have to think about someone else being able to repeat it. It's easy to design something that has 49 colors in it, but most people aren't going to be able to afford to or be inclined to make it. I have a piece in my closet right now that I couldn't figure out how to explain to people how to make it so they would understand. My work has had to be reasonable for someone to repeat.

What do you look for in the yarns you choose for your work?

For me, the design of the yarn itself is the important thing—color in secondary. I like yarns that have structure and loft, which gives it a lightness that helps to hold up the stitch pattern so it doesn't sag. I prefer single ply over a plied yarn that tends to reflect light in a way that distracts from the stitch pattern.

I also like rustic yarns to a certain extent. What I look for is character in the yarn, which I usually call ego. You have to take into consideration what the yarn will do. The design of the Noro yarns, with their color being secondary to me, are just perfect, in my opinion.

With my own yarns, I'm finally there where I have textures that work well together to do what I want to do.

There is a certain sincerity that comes across in the way you show your work. Where does that come from?

I do my own photography for my work. I use real people, not models, because my customers are real people. I like to show women in a softer, more beautiful way, and I need to be inspired by the person to make it work right.

Spending your time between Atlanta and Sweden, two very different parts of the world., what is your ideal environment for creating?

It's safe to say that I would not have the career that I have if I had stayed in New York, where I started. In Sweden, you have a long period of the year where there's no green, there's winter, so the colors of the yarn are very riveting. The quiet of the Swedish winters really helped me along. Sweden allowed me to have the time and the vision to create.

In Atlanta, you have nature, and you can go out and do things. You don't want to stay indoors all the time. Where I lived in Sweden, there's not much to do, so I was happy to sit home and knit. Here in the US, you have so much to do on a daily basis, and you have to keep a lot of balls in the air.

In Sweden, you kind of have your life sorted out for you, so there's more time to apply to something else.

Who has inspired you most in your career?

The designer, Norah Gaughan, is one whose work I have admired. I talked to her one day, and we talked about how our brains work in the same way.

Apparently, we are more mathematical, and yet, I have the whimsical too. That's the balance again.

I tend to follow my own advice. One thing often comes at the cost of another thing. Maybe if I did go to design school, it would have helped me in a different way, but I guess my problem is that I'm too independent. I like figuring things out, and I'm willing to make the mistakes. I like teamwork when it comes to photoshoots and so forth, but the best advice I ever gave myself was to be independent of a company's influence. I had to do my own thing.

Otherwise, I don't look at a lot of other people's work. Even when I travel, I like to just take things as they come.

What is the best advice you've ever been given?

I didn't go to art or design school. I did take a creative writing course; I was an English literature major. There was a lot of, "Well, you have to do it this way" or "You have to do it that way." I didn't want that. As a result, I never did anything with creative writing again.

Use of a deflected warp and Brooks Bouquet accents evoke texture, openwork, and balance as inspired by the work of Cornelia Tuttle Hamilton.

The Trilia Shawl

A variety of silks and a touch of mohair add elegance to this textured shawl. The symmetrical patterns at each end serve as focal points. Alternatively, you can weave the pickup pattern continuously between the openwork to heighten the textured effect.

Somewhere along the way, I read that the name Trilia came from relying less on your peers and more on your own powers - appropriate to the theme of this chapter.

Finished Measurements approximately 13" (33 cm) W x 65"(165 cm) L

Equipment

- Rigid heddle loom with 15" (38 cm) weaving width
- 8 dent reed
- 1 shuttle
- 2 pick-up sticks
- Fringe twister (optional)

Warp

1 skein each of the following 2 Hamilton Yarns:

Silke in Plum, 100% mulberry silk, 100 gm = 252 yds (230 m). Uses 32 yds (29.5 m).

Silkette in Savannah, 100% mulberry silk, 50 gm = 153 yds (140 m). Uses 105 yds (97 m).

2 Skeins Hamilton Yarns Sister Silk in Falu Red, 100% hand-dyed mulberry silk, 50 gm = 131 yds (120 m). Uses 215 yds (196.5 m).

Weft

1 skein Hamilton Yarns Affetto Seta in Lava, 70% kid mohair / 30% silk, 50 gm = 262 yds (240 m). Uses 245 yds (225 m).

Sett: 8 epi, 10 ppi in plain weave, 13 ppi in pattern weave

To have the contrast loop of Silke accent the center of the deflected warp sections and the "windowpane" of the Brooks Bouquet, we require it to be in a hole with an equal count of odd numbers of warp ends between each loop of that yarn. You can use a warping board or use my direct warp method that follows.

Warp

14" (35.5 cm) W x 94" (239) L = 112 ends according to the Diagrams A-D that follow. These look more complicated than they really are. Here's how to use them: Each drawing represents a warped section of your reed with white heddles with holes and shaded spaces representing slots. Each yarn is represented by a color, as shown in the key above the diagrams.

The shorter vertical bars are loops you will draw into slots as you face the back of the loom. The longer vertical lines are loops you will draw into holes. Under the diagrams, I've written the number of loops to draw before each Silke loop. Note the shift from drawing loops into slots to drawing into holes and the corresponding change to the loop count.

Alternating between 8 and 7 loops will set us up to sley an uneven number of single strands between each Silke contrast loop, as you will see on the next page.

When you complete one repeat of Diagram A, continue leftward, starting on the right side of Diagram B for the center stripes. Complete this sequence two times, as noted in the green bar across the top.

Finally, work Diagram C one time from right to left, and you are done drawing the loops.

▌ = Sister Silk ▌ = Silke ▌ = Silkette

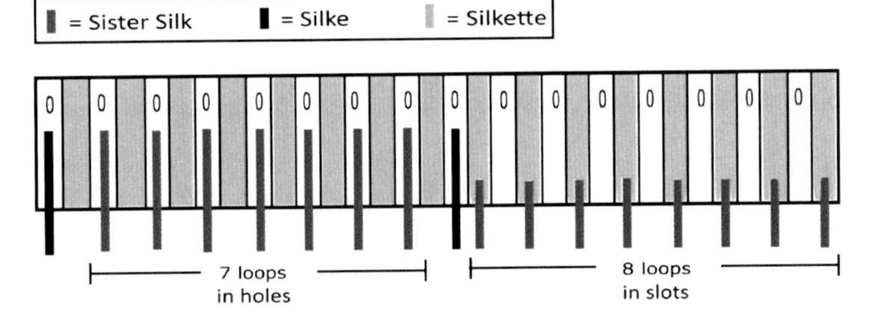

Diagram A - starting at right, complete for the right border

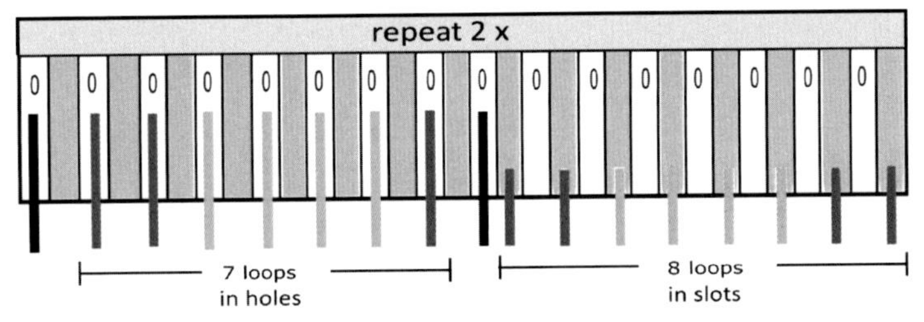

Diagram B - center color changes continuing right to left. Cut and tie off at the color changes between Sister Silk and Silkette.

Diagram C - ending left border

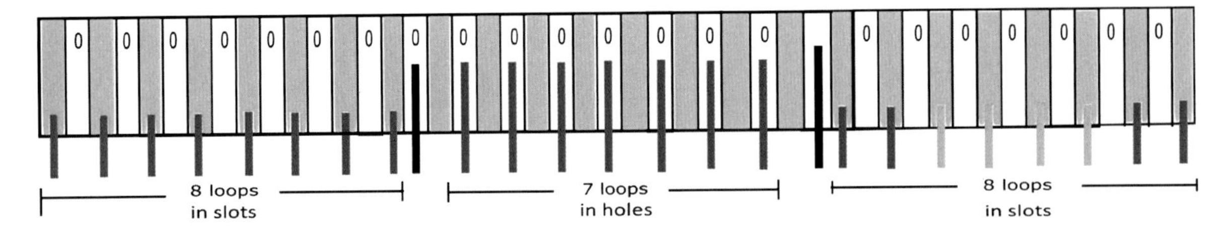

Sley the reed: Diagram D below is provided to give you a visual of the result after sleying the reed. You are now looking at the front of your loom, so the drawings are reversed. I've joined Diagrams A-C together to represent the full width of the warp. This time the vertical lines represent single ends. Don't focus too intently on this diagram.

You really only need to know three things here:

1. Sley to the empty slot or hole to the right.
2. At the left side of every other Silke loop, you will move one end from that slot to the slot on the other side of the Silke (where it is marked with arrows).
3. The Silke loop stays put as double strands in a hole.

This puts 15 ends between every Silke loop except for the section at the right with 16 ends.

Wind on and tie the ends onto the front apron rod as usual.

ey into the slot or hole to the right across.

Diagram D

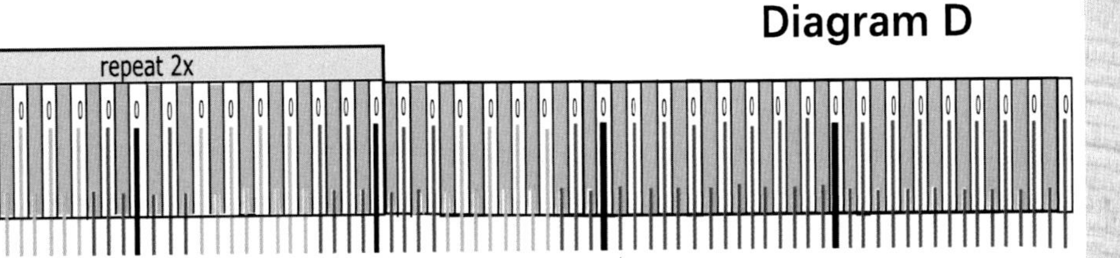

Set the 2 pick-up sticks

Place the heddle in the down position.

Working with the warp ends of the upper row (these are slot threads) behind the reed:

Set pick-up stick B by picking up the first warp end, skip over the 2nd, pick up the 3rd, and skip over the 4th. Then pick up *the next 4 warp ends, skip over 4. Repeat from * across to the last 4 ends. Pick up 1, skip over 1, pick up 1, skip over 1.

Set pick-up stick A by skipping over the first warp end, pick up the 2nd, skip over the 3rd, and pick up the 4th. Then skip over *the next 4 warp ends, pick up 4. Repeat from * across to the last 4 ends. Skip over 1, pick up 1, skip over 1, pick up 1. These are the opposite of ends picked up by B.

Weave

using Affeto Seta throughout according to the weaving order at right. See chart reading p. 10 if you need help reading the chart.
Starting with heddle up and on the right side, work each weave from the top to the bottom of this chart. Weave 47"(cm) in plain weave, then repeat the chart from the bottom upward to complete approximately 70" of weaving. Deflected warp and Brooks Bouquet instructions are on the next page. The weaving order chart below shows the number of repeats (reps) for the special weaves and the number of picks for plain weave in between.

Deflected Warp Weave	Brooks Bouquet	Plain Weave
		4 picks
3 reps		
		4 picks
	1 rep	
		4 picks
1-1/2 reps		
		4 picks
	1 rep	
3 reps		

Deflected Warp using 2 Pick-up Sticks

Set two pick-up sticks as described in the box on p. 91. If you need advice on pick-up patterns, see p. 11.

You will need to remove pick-up stick A after each 8 step repeat and place it again before starting another A sequence. B can remain in place throughout. Start with A as follows:

Step 1. Heddle Up

Step 2. Pick up stick A forward and up at the reed

Step 3. Heddle Up

Step 4. Pick up stick A forward and up at the reed

Step 5. Heddle Up

Step 6. Pick up stick A forward and up at the reed

Step 7. Heddle Up

Step 8. Heddle Down

Remove A and follow the same 8 steps for B.

The entire A and B sequence is one repeat.

The deflected warp results in a wavy pattern as the warp ends are pulled in opposite directions with the alternation of pick-up sticks A and B. This may not be apparent until the weaving is removed from the loom.

Figure 1

Brooks Bouquet on an Open Shed With Modified Selvages

You will need a stable margin at the sides of this open weave for seaming the pillow. I'll call the ends between the Silke yarn "sections," To get a plain weave border, weave 6 picks on the first and last sections only. This is the first 16 ends on the right, and the last 15 ends at the left selvage (total of upper and lower ends in the open shed). You will need to add a 12" (30.5 cm) long strand of weft at the left side to weave each border simultaneously. Weave in the extra weft tails as you go.

At right, when the 6 pick borders are done, insert the shuttle into the next shed past the border just woven, under the following 8 upper ends (the Silke loop counts as one) to exit out of the top of the warp. *Insert the shuttle back into the shed 7 upper ends back. You are working up to each Silke loop to surround the 7 warp ends between them. Pass the shuttle onward through the shed to exit through the top on the far side of the next section (15 upper ends from where you just inserted). Cinch the bundle you just wrapped tightly to form an hourglass shape. Below you will see a close-up of the plain weave border at the pillow edge in Figure 1.

Work from * across. Do not surround the last section. Instead, pass the shuttle through the remainder of the shed and out the left end.

Now weave a 6 pick border at the first and last sections again.

This time, working the shuttle on the left, you will lay in a 12" (30.5 cm) strand of weft from the left of the first section so you can weave this simultaneously and in the same direction as the left border. Tuck weft tails as you weave.

Figure 2

Resume plain weave across.

For the Trilia shawl, I just raised thc first pick of the Brooks Bouquet by about 1/2" (1.5 cm), started wrapping on the 2nd section, and exited without wrapping the last section to lessen the draw-in at the edge. You can choose to do what I did, wrap that first and last section, or border it as with the pillow.

Finish

Remove from the loom tying 4 strand tassels. You can twist them as I did below. Wash according to method one, p. 12.

Twisted Fringe

I tend to prefer fringe in its natural state, but certain yarns unply easily and look unruly left on their own. If you would like to twist your fringe, as shown in our shawl, a fringe twisting device is indispensable to speed up a task that can be very tedious.

My fringe twister has 3 alligator clips in case you want to twist together 3 paired strands. Here I used 2 of them.

Anchor your shawl with a weight or tape it to a surface with painter's or cellophane tape so it doesn't slide around as you work across.

Attach 2 fringe strands to each clip and twist in one direction, pulling the strands straight. Count the number of times you turn the handle to get consistency across.

Now, pinching the ends so they don't unwind, tie the twisted strands together at the end with an overhand knot. The strands will wind back on themselves to secure the twist.

Noro yarns have an earthy quality that results in a beautiful fabric. Because they are softly spun single ply, they break too easily to be used extensively as warp. That doesn't stop us from adding an isolated loop of this yarn between stronger warp threads to accent the warp and use it as weft.

The Trilia Pillow

Here's a quick project to liven up your living space or give as a gift.

To give a background to the open weave, I upcycled a fabric-covered pillow I had on hand that coordinated with my yarn colors. I chose to complete the back side in plain weave for a different look on each side.

Finished Measurements approximately 16" (42 cm) square

Equipment and Materials

- Rigid heddle loom with at least 18" (46 cm) weaving width
- 8 dent reed
- 1 stick shuttle
- 2 - pick-up sticks
- Hair pick or tapestry beater for edge weaving with Brooks Bouquet
- 18" (46 cm) fabric-covered pillow in a solid color that coordinates with your yarn choice. The fabric will be visible through the open weave at the center front.
- Sewing machine to sew pillow case
- Needle and thread to hand stitch the pillow case closed

Warp and Weft - 1 ball of Noro Ito in color 19, 100% wool, 200 gm = 437 yds (399 m). Uses 190 yds (174 m). I had enough left over from the Patchwork Vest, p. 52 to complete this pillow. Any of the Noro yarns in a worsted or aran gauge will work as well.

Warp - 2 skeins Hikoo CoBaSi Dk in Natural Olive, 55% Cotton, 16% Bamboo, 8% Silk, 21% Elastic Nylon, 50 gm = 140 yds (128 m). Uses 227 yds (208 m).

Sett: 8 epi x 8 ppi in plain weave, 10 ppi in pattern weave

Once seamed, the pillow case will end up about 1-1/2" smaller than the 18" pillow for a snug fit to avoid sagging.

Warp

18" W x 60" L = 144 ends where the double strand of Ito counts as **1,** according to Diagram A and B that follow. If you made the Trilia scarf, you are already a pro at reading these. If not, here's what you do for direct warping:

Each drawing represents the warped section of your reed with white heddles with holes and shaded spaces representing slots. Starting with Diagram A, each yarn is represented by a color, as shown in the key below. The shorter vertical bars are loops you will draw into slots as you face the back of the loom. The longer vertical lines are loops you will draw into holes.

Under those, I've written the number of loops to draw before each Silke loop. Note the shift from drawing loops into slots to drawing into holes and the corresponding change to the loop count.

Alternating between 8 and 7 loops will set us up to sley an uneven number of single strands between each Silke contrast loop.

In Diagram B, the vertical bars are now single strands to show you what it looks like once you sley the reed. That drawing is the reverse of A because you are now facing the front of the loom. You don't need to study this too closely. Simply sley to the empty slot or hole to the right. At the left side of every other Silke loop, you will move one end from that slot to the slot on the other side of the Silke (where it is marked with an arrow). The Silke loops remain as a double strand in the hole.

This puts 15 ends between every Silke loop except for the final section at the right (Diagram B) with 16 ends.

Wind on and tie the ends onto the front apron rod as usual.

Diagram A

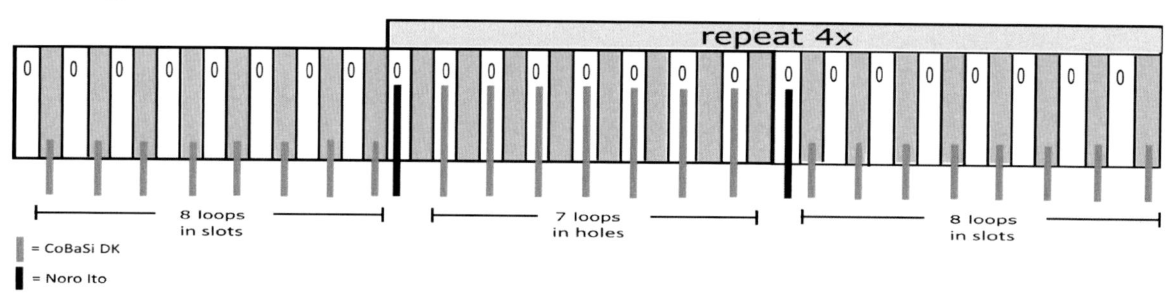

Diagram B

whether starting at right or left, sley into slot or hole to the right across.

repeat 4x

Weave

with Ito according to the weaving order chart at right, reading top downward. See directions for chart reading p. 10. Plain weave is given by measurement, and the special weaves are given in the number of repeats.

Keep track of your total weaving length. You can adjust the amount of plain weave at the end to weave a total length of 36" (91.5 cm).

Directions for the Deflected Warp weave and the Brooks Bouquet with Modified Selvages are on p. 92. The selvages need to be stable for seaming. Below is a photo showing the built-up the selvages with a supplemental weft on the loom.

Deflected Warp Weave	Brooks Bouquet	Plain Weave
		3 in/ 8cm
3 reps		
	1 rep	
1-1/2 reps		
	1 rep	
3 reps		
		21 in/ 53 cm

Finishing

Weave a footer and cut from the loom. Raw finish each end (see p. 18). Wash according to method two, p. 12.

Assemble

Fold the case in half with right sides together. Sew the selvage sides together with 3/8" (1 cm) seam allowance. Check the width and length of the case before sewing to see if you should adjust the seam allowance. The finished width and length should be around 16-1/2" (42 cm) square.

Next, fold the raw edges down 5/8" (1.6 cm) around the top (wrong sides together). Press in place and stitch 1/4" (.5 cm) from the open edge around.

Turn the case right side out and stuff the fabric-covered pillow inside. Hand stitch the case shut at the top with needle and thread using a figure 8 stitch, described on p. 169.

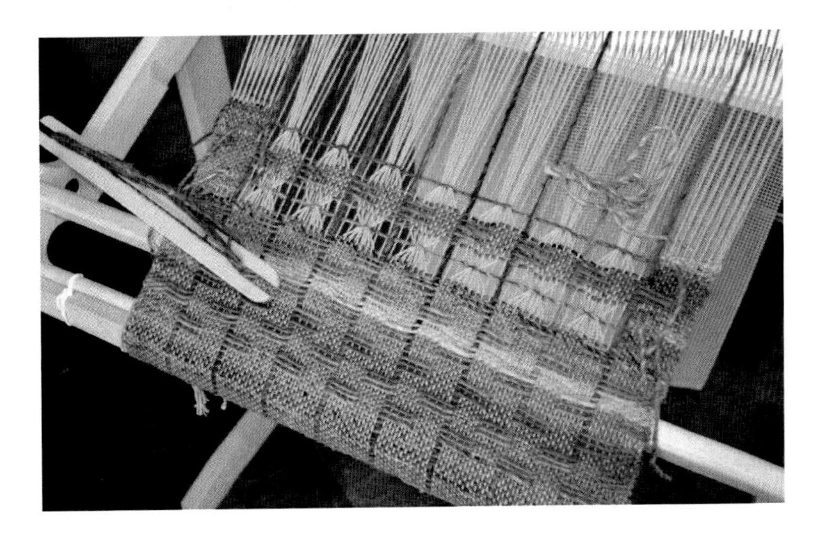

Chapter 5

> **"If one could only catch that true color of nature - the very thought of it drives me mad."**
>
> **- Andrew Wyeth**

"Mere color can speak to the soul in a thousand different ways."
- Oscar Wilde

There is a strong link between our emotions and color. In my 2nd book, *Color and Texture for the Rigid Heddle Loom*, I present the following list of colors and their associated effect:

Red - excitement, passion, joy, aggression

Orange - joy, warmth, happiness, freedom

Yellow - cheerfulness, optimism, intellect, fear

Blue - peace, coolness, sincerity, depression

Green - calm, nature, hope, envy

Purple and Violet - deep feeling, loyalty, luxury, death

Pink - playful, feminine, sensual, tranquil

Brown - dreary, earthy, grounding, honest

Beige - calm, relaxing, dependable, conservative

The frequency of a color's wavelength can have a physical effect on our senses and is the source in part for our response. Our reaction to color is also influenced by culture and can vary person-to-person based upon our experience.

Red, for example, is usually the color of excitement or urgency. However, if it was the color of your childhood home, it may be associated with warmth or comfort to you. In South Africa, red holds many meanings, including love and beauty. If you are Chinese, you might wear red on the New Year or to a wedding or a funeral. In China, red is associated with luck, prosperity, happiness, and long life.

The many Indie dyers (independent dyers not associated with a large company) I've worked with have a deep respect for the significance of color. They are not unlike the ancient alchemists.

Merriam-Webster writes that, "Alchemists believed that lead could be 'perfected' into gold, that diseases could be cured, and that life could be prolonged through transmutation or a change of some essential element into a superior form."

The superior form that the independent dyer brings to yarn grants us a unique range of tonal and multi-color opportunities to enrich our weaving.

My next artist brings color to life inspired by her travels across the beautiful countryside of her home state of Wisconsin.

As you read on, think about what color means to you and how this awareness can add meaning to your work.

Tracey Schuh

I represented Interlacements Yarn as a wholesale rep for their independent dye studio from 2010 (shortly after Tracey and Jim Schuh bought the company) through 2014. I have known her as both a collaborative partner and a friend during and since that time. Everyone who knows Tracey will testify that she is a kind-hearted and good-natured person - a treasure to know.

Tracey is a resident of Abrams, Wisconsin, where she invites friends, family, and fiber enthusiasts from around the US to join her in her love of spinning, weaving, and knitting with classes and events. She's also a devoted grandmother, seldom pictured without one of her grandchildren as in the delightful photo your see at right.

I caught up with Tracey as she was nearing the completion of chemo treatments for cancer. I was pleased to hear she has achieved full remission. We look forward to hearing so much more from her as she continues to explore new yarns.

Interlacements Yarns is known for bright, clear colors on rayon and wool. Their Zig Zag yarn is a unique rayon crepe that I use frequently in my work It produces an extraordinary drape with a subtle sheen - great for garments.

Learn more about Tracey, her yarns, and patterns at www.interlacementsyarns.com.

Your hand-dyed yarns are known for their vibrancy and clarity. What has influenced your color choices as you have grown the Interlacements brand?

At first, it was just the color, but as I got into it more, it was feelings and memories and things put into the color. As an example, my mom and I created the Indian Camp colorway together from a place that we used to go to in Colorado. It was known as a lookout or camp that Native Americans used. We took the color of the sky and the bluff and the trees – the real southwestern tones and turned that into a colorway. That is really something I like.

We have quite a few of the Door County, Wisconsin colors. There's Egg Harbor, Ephraim, Sister Bay, Liberty Grove, Sturgeon Bay. I'm probably missing a couple there. Door county is kind of a little fingertip that goes up the east side of Wisconsin. It's well known for vacationers with neat little shops and lots of artists. It's always nice to go up there and do some research, eat a little of the food, and yeah...it's great.

What does a typical day looks like in your studio?

I do full kettles unless I'm not feeling up to it. I probably have twenty big kettles. I work in a six-car garage that I've completely taken over.

Views of Egg Harbor, Wisconsin

We have more of the office up in the house than it used to be. It has definitely grown.

So if I get out there around 9 a.m., I'll have maybe six kettles going. That's kind of a small, normal day. By noon, I'm pretty close to being done. It just has to process. I leave it overnight. I find that I get more of a vibrant color if I don't rinse right away. When I've done classes, and we've had to rinse right away so my students can take their skeins home, the colors are lighter.

The next morning when I get up, Jim's got them rinsed and out on the dryer racks for me. He likes to say he retired so he could go to work for me. He does all the driving to the shows and all the cooking too. I know, I'm spoiled.

There are a couple of mills that will wind for me. Some won't wind large enough, or some won't wind small enough. I like big skeins. I like messing around with one skein, not twenty -five skeins.

When I need to wind, my husband Jim is my winder. He'll stand at the winder for five to six hours and get me loaded up. Then I'll blast through the yarn. I can dye faster than he can wind.

Is your process different for wool than for rayon?

There's not a huge difference between dyeing wool and dyeing rayon. To me, wool is easy. It's like baby steps. First, you do the wool. The cottons and rayons take a little more finesse. When I do a show, I'll look down the aisle, and everyone will have wools and silks, wools and blends, and there won't be anybody with cottons and rayons. I like being different.

Your website mentions that you are always trying new and inventive ways to apply the dye. What are some of the things you have learned with this experimentation?

I have learned that if I don't wear gloves, I get looked at very strangely. I'll have blue and purple on the underpart of my arm here that I've missed. I'll go into a store, or worse, chemo, and they'll say, "Ohh, what happened to you!" I have learned that I have to wear gloves and keep them on because my hands want to get in there and mess around.

Also, my natural lighting has changed. My dye studio is very well lit. I like having the big doors open so that I can let the light in. I dry outside in the summer because I love it. There's nothing like driving up my driveway and seeing those racks out. It's gorgeous.

You are an active participant in fiber events. How much does this networking play a role in your art?

It's huge. People like to come into the booth, show me what they have made, wearing what they have made, which I love. I've made so many friends from all over – not just from the US, but some have come from Europe as well. We have actually stayed with some of them afterward, done stuff, gone out to eat.

My network has definitely influenced my colors. Years ago, everyone strayed away from yellow tones. Like, "Oh, Michigan doesn't like yellow tones" or "doesn't like orange." I kept hearing that over and over and kept thinking, "Why? They're such pretty colors." I've taken

Toasty Toes Indian Camp

some of the colors they like and just try to blend in the yellow a little bit or put something next to it that made it just pop right out. That has worked really well. I've got some yarns now that have the yellow tones in them, and they have been really hot sellers.

I also have yarn shops that have requested their own specific colors. I have a yarn shop up in Baileys Harbor that I let choose their own colors. I had her go to a paint store and get paint chips and put them in the order that she wanted to see them. She did a fabulous job, and it has been a great colorway. I have had five or six shops now request their own color.

Recent upheaval in our economy and social order have combined with changing demographics to challenge the craft industry. The local yarn shop is becoming harder to find. How do you see this affecting the fiber craft community?

We see it by the online shopping increasing and the wholesale orders to yarn shop orders decreasing. I hate it. I miss my yarn shops. I miss talking with them. I miss putting on promotions with them. People cannot touch or feel those skeins online. They can't see them in natural lighting. I can do everything under the sun to try to get a good picture, but it is just not the same.

The age group of our customers is still about the same. I don't see a lot of eighteen-year-olds or younger. Our yarns are a little more costly than Walmart yarns. I tend to get a slightly older crowd that has a little better income. It's funny because I have had people who have used my yarns for thirty years. It hasn't gotten old for them. Nothing has changed that they are not still buying.

Love for your work comes through clearly in your public profile. What advice might you offer fiber enthusiasts to stay in love with their work?

Always try something new. You have sort of turned the world upside down with your rigid heddle, and I see it going a zillion different ways now. It's not just about the color. It's about the texture. It's about the feel. It's about the way it makes you feel when you are working with it.

I love what I do. I have to say, with this COVID -19 and not being able to get out with the cancer and everything, I am more content staying at home than most people have been. I have the biggest yarn stash in the world. Because I spin, I weave, I knit, boredom is not in my vocabulary. I'm always trying something new. I go on YouTube to see what else is out there – what did I miss?

I have a good life and an excellent husband. I don't know what I would do without him. When Judy (the previous owner of Interlacements) called me and said she was ill and it was terminal, I was crying. I was losing a friend. Jim walked in, and when I explained to him what was happening, he said, "Call her back and tell her we will buy it." I have never regretted acquiring this business, and I haven't looked back a day since.

One great way to show off the brilliant hues of Interlacements yarns is to frame them with black as in this colorful Ruana.

Rayon Ruana

Multi-directional stripes color this flexible piece that can hang down the front or drape gracefully to the side. This one is simple to weave, quick to assemble, and works well in all seasons.

Finished Measurements approximately 58" (147.5 cm) long from back to front edges to hang 29" (73.5 cm) from shoulder. Right and left panels are approximately 18-1/2" (47 cm) wide

Equipment

- Loom with at least 21" (53.5 cm) weaving width
- 10 dent reed
- 3 shuttles
- Sewing machine and black thread
- Straight pins

Warp and Weft

3 skeins Interlacements ZigZag in Black, 100% rayon, 8 oz. = 500 yds (457 m). Uses 1206 yds (1103 m).

Warp

1 skein Interlacements Zig Zag in Violet. Uses 218 yds (199.5 m).

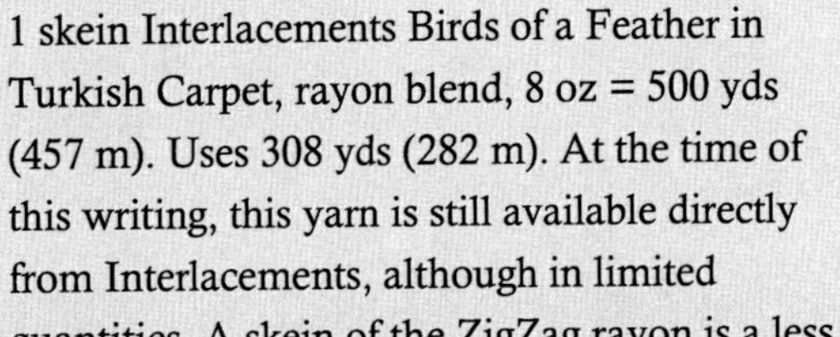

1 skein Interlacements Birds of a Feather in Turkish Carpet, rayon blend, 8 oz = 500 yds (457 m). Uses 308 yds (282 m). At the time of this writing, this yarn is still available directly from Interlacements, although in limited quantities. A skein of the ZigZag rayon is a less textural but perfect substitute.

10 epi, 8-9 ppi

You will warp 2 times as follows:

Warp Main Pieces

21" (53.5 cm) W x 104" (264 cm) L = 210 ends, according to chart A below. See chart reading p. 10. Black and Violet indicate the 2 colors of ZigZag. Birds is Birds of a Feather or Zig Zag in Turkish Carpet.

Chart A

12		12		26		6		26		12		12	Black
	16				22		22				16		Birds
			14						14				Violet

Weave Main Pieces **(make 2)**

using Zig Zag in black for 40" (101.5 cm). Weave 2 picks of a contrast scrap yarn, cutting and tucking ending and beginning tails, and weave the 2nd piece of equal length. A black weft enhances the richness of the warp colors.

When the 2nd piece is complete, weave a footer and cut from the loom.

Warp End Pieces

13-1/4" (34.5 cm) W x 112" (284.5 cm) L = 132 ends according to Chart B below.

Chart B

16		14		14		16	Black
			28				Birds
	22				22		Violet

Weave End Pieces

(make 4) using Zig Zag in black for 22" (56 cm). Weave 2 picks of a contrast scrap yarn, and weave the 3 more piece of equal length, cutting and tucking ending and beginning tails.

When the 4th piece is complete, weave a footer and cut from the loom.

Finish

Raw finish all ends, p. 18. Wash according to method one for hand-dyed yarn, p. 12.

Assemble

The diagram below represents the finished ruana laid flat

Pin a selvage of each end piece to each raw finish edge of the two main pieces, right sides together. You should find that the end pieces are slightly longer than the main piece widths to allow for weaving differences. If you line up one side, you can trim the other edge to fit perfectly. Stitch the seam first (with 1/2" allowance), then raw finish and trim the excess from one side of each end piece.

Press the seam allowances away from the main pieces. On the right side, topstitch 1/4" (.5 cm) away from the

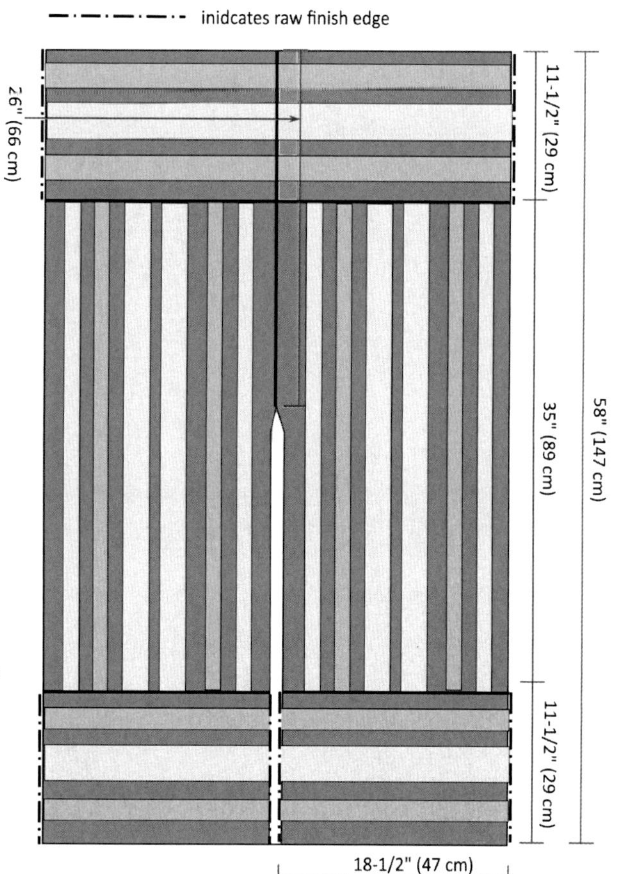

seam through all thicknesses.

Pin the assembled panels with right sides together, matching the stripes of the end pieces on one end. See p. 19 for matching stripes.

Sew a 26" (66 cm) long skinny seam (2 warp ends wide) from the bottom upward for the back center join. Backstitch at the top of the seam to secure this edge. Reinforce the opening by staystitching, p. 19.

Your ruana is ready to wear.

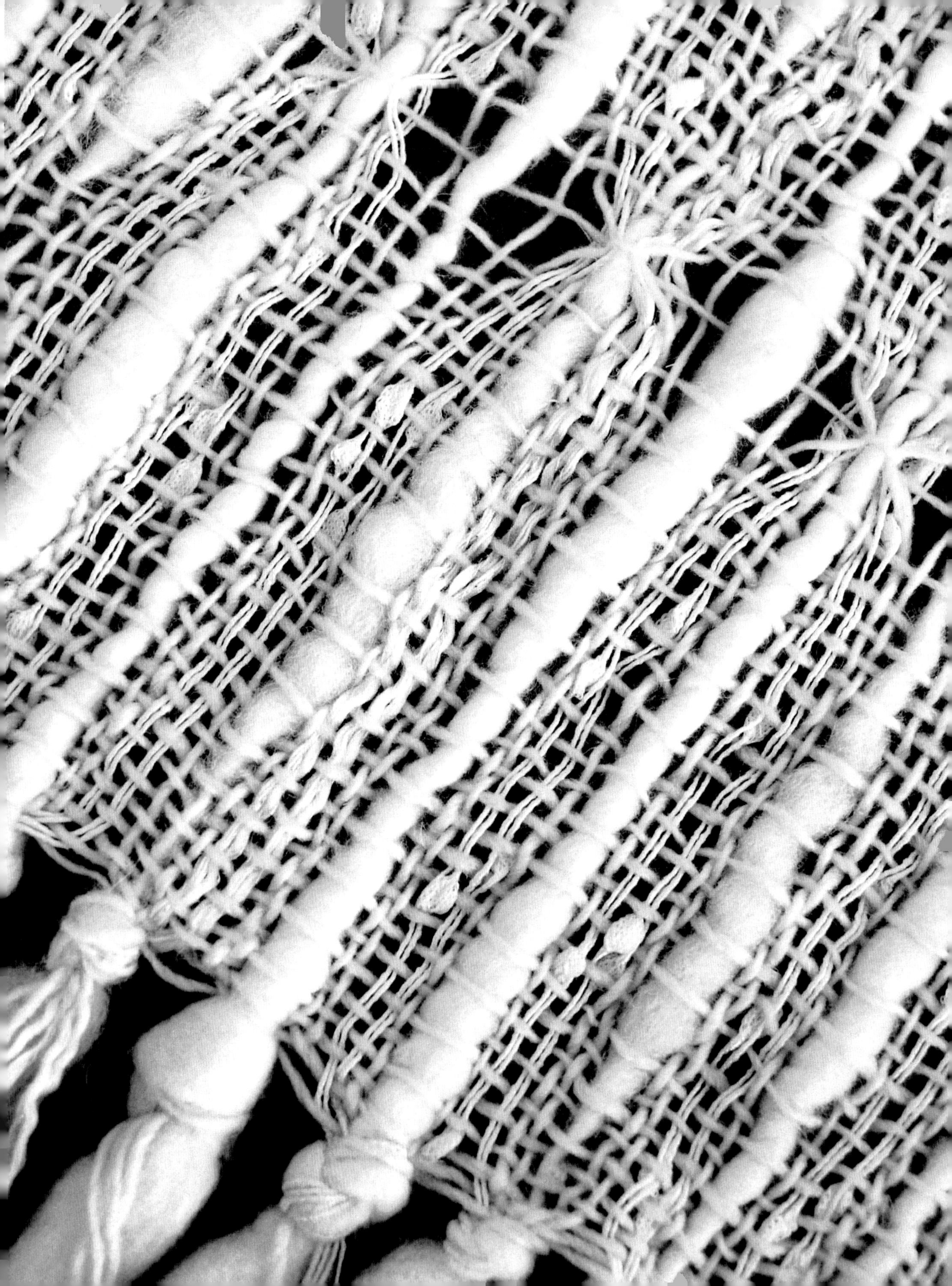

Chapter 6

Stay Motivated

"Inhale possibility,
exhale creativity."
– Laura Jaworski

"Inspiration can come to us at any time and from many sources."

-Jim Rohn

Over the years that I have taught rigid heddle weaving, I've had many students tell me how thrilled they were to learn this craft. Some have struggled with other yarn crafts, sometimes due to coordination problems, medical complications, or attention span issues. The accessibility of our loom has broadened its appeal.

I also hear from students who almost gave up learning rigid heddle, who preserved and are now teaching others. I find this very rewarding.

Then again, I've followed up with many aspiring weavers who have decided they just don't feel like weaving anymore. Somewhere along the way, they lost momentum.

What brings us to the rigid heddle in the first place? For many, it is all about the love of fiber - getting your hands dirty with yarn. It's not that we lose that; it's that life gets in the way. Once that loom goes deep into the closet, too often, motivation goes with it.

Staying in touch with inspiration starts with removing barriers. After all the weaving I've done, the thing that still holds me back is getting started - getting the loom out with all its setup, preparing the yarn, and drawing the first loop.

I've taken a close look at that problem and modified my surroundings to minimize it. I realized that I like to weave in the living room, finish and sew in the kitchen, and design in the dining room. The simple response was to make my looms a part of the living room décor, install a cabinet in the kitchen to hold my sewing machine plus a washtub with soap bottle and towels, and integrate a desk and computer into the dining room. I even keep a warping peg attached discretely to the edge of a living room side table and include equipment in the decor to minimize setup.

With barriers reduced, I'm ready to go to work when the muse strikes.

My next artist, Mona Muhammad, draws her inspiration by embracing input from others and the materials of her trade. I love how she gives life to her yarn by asking it to show her the way. For her, to stay motivated is to stay curious. She lives with an openness to ideas to process and interpret new and unique creations in crochet.

Mona Muhammad

When I discovered Mona Muhammad, owner of KnottyLoop, I knew nothing about her. Still, her stunning, fashion-forward designs spoke volumes, so I jumped at the chance to include her here. I was thrilled to learn more about this innovative and energetic woman in our interview. I found her to both generous with her time as well as her thoughts.

Mona offers stylish crocheted ready-to-wear and custom garments for all body types on Etsy.com. Her collection is as expansive as her enthusiasm is contagious. I found it interesting that her direction came to her as a flash of insight. It has kept her going creatively for many years, making her perfect for this chapter on staying motivated.

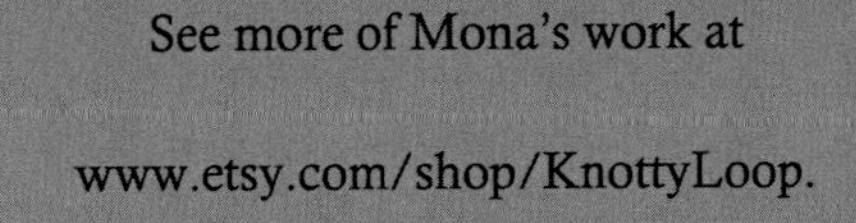

See more of Mona's work at

www.etsy.com/shop/KnottyLoop.

When we look at your Etsy shop, we see that you are a prolific designer, but it doesn't tell us anything about you. Please tell our readers a little about what led you to become a crochet designer.

Like most people, I learned from my mother and my grandmother. My mother was my biggest teacher. She taught me the value of starting things over. I used to hate it when I was a kid. I would start something and take it to her and say, "Look what I did." She would say, "Well, you messed up your stitches right about there." I remember very clearly. I liked to sit on the floor. I still do. I would sit on the floor and have to pull it all out. I was happy with what I did, but I learned how to make very neat stitches. I'm grateful to her now because she is a big part of what I have done.

Later, my daughter-in-law and I were peeking through a magazine that came in the mail. She said to me, "I like this crochet dress, but, oh, it's so expensive." I said to her, "I think I can make that." Now I had not crocheted for a few years, other than a few things I had made for my kids when they were growing up. They outgrew that. They wanted to go to the mall to get their stuff. They wanted the same name brands that their friends were wearing. Now when they come to me to create something, it really makes me very proud.

My daughter-in-law kind of dared me, so I ended up making that piece for her. I also made pieces for my four sisters. They started wearing them out, and then their friends started calling. Originally, I was crocheting for them by request where they would buy the yarn, and I would make the piece. About that time, I was doing customer service, and I switched companies. Money was a little tight for a minute, so this became a second source of income for me.

I remember when I was invited to do my first fundraiser fashion show. The models were in a room getting dressed. I was completely terrified. I was standing in the hallway, against the wall, and I basically could not breathe, could not talk. I was just waiting for this thing to be over. I remember I was thinking, "Oh, people are going to laugh me off the stage." Instead, I got a standing ovation. It let me know that I was on the right path.

Have you pursued other outlets for your work besides your Etsy shop, and, if so, how do they compare?

I do a lot of vendor shows (i.e., shows focused on direct sales and business connections). I started

out doing craft shows, but they weren't very profitable for me. What they were looking for was mostly crafty things, discounted things. What I was doing was dealing mostly with fashion. So I found vendor shows focused on clothing lines, home fashions, etc.

I've also had my work in a couple of boutiques. Those do pretty well for me. Facebook, Instagram, social media outlets have been good to put my work out there.

The designs you create are bold, sexy, and fashion-conscious. Who or what has influenced your style?

There are multiple sources that inspire me. I can be out shopping or see something on a website, and I will wonder how I can translate what I see into crochet. Also, I can meet somebody and get a feel for their style. I can create by just looking at the dimensions of their body. Many times clients will come here, and I will be able to say, "That style will look good on a size 8. It won't work on a size 14, but we can do this...

I'm proud to say that my designs are my designs. I enjoy going on Pinterest. I also love looking at YouTube – their runway shows. This may tell me what colors or styles are popular for the year. I love to look at designers that go over the top, but their design is not for me. When I create something, it has to be a practical, wearable piece.

The yarn probably influences me more than anything else. I look at the yarn and think, "How is this going to flow." Maybe it would make a great poncho or a great jumpsuit vs. it making a great dress. Then I look at how things will feel against the skin. Some yarns will hug you, yet some yarns will have a touch of a scratch, so that yarn would be better where someone could wear a slip or something under it. I get a few requests for wool, but 90% of my clients want to stay away from animal fibers because of the itch factor or because of allergies.

What do you think about when you begin a new design?

I don't mean to be insulting, because some people really like the old style of crochet. There are so many yarns out there to give you so many options right now. Crochet can be lighter. Crochet can flow. It doesn't have to be that heavy, patterned, granny square, one way to look anymore. I look for yarns that can give flow that will complement the body in a certain way. If someone has a body issue, say a midsection that they want to hide, or they're top-heavy, I look for ways to camouflage that.

Even if I do a granny square jacket, I look for ways to make it look light. When you turn, it should turn with you and not be sitting back there after you've made your turn.

My mother was big into blankets. She'd sit there for four or five weeks, putting together her squares with the flowers on top. It used to drive me crazy. Don't get me wrong. I love those blankets. I still have them. When my mother was alive (she lived with me for the last two years of her life), she said to me, "Where did you learn how to do this?" I said, "You taught me." She said, "I taught you how to crochet. I never taught you how to do this." I think about that sometimes. Whatever she taught me, this grew from that.

What keeps you motivated and inspires you to create new ideas?

When I first started crocheting things for people, I was looking at patterns, but it was repetitive. I didn't want to get into making the same thing over 200 times. I wanted to design a dress. I guess that was weighing heavy on my mind because, one night, I went to bed, and I dreamed about what I wanted to make. I got up that day, I called off from work, and I finished that dress that day. It was my first really original design from beginning to end. From that point, the designs have not stopped.

I love what I do. I enjoy collecting yarn. I bought some yarn yesterday, and I don't need to buy yarn (ever). It's a new yarn, and I can't wait. When I'm finished talking with you, I'm going to go upstairs and see which way the yarn takes me.

I'm not sure how we're going to end up, but I want to do something different than I've done before. The whole thing is not to be afraid of where the yarn is going to take you.

Sometimes I'll start on a piece with something in mind, and I'll think, "Huh, I wonder what would happen if I went left instead of right?" Sometimes the models who walk for me, that I don't even know, inspire the next design. I go to some of these fashion shows, and they say, "Here are your ten models." I'll give them a piece to wear, and it's a standard dress, off the shoulder or whatever. Sometimes they come back with something totally different. They put it on as a skirt or pull it all the way up as a neckpiece. So I'll think, "What if I put a piece of elastic here, and I did this or that, it would work permanently." I appreciate what they do.

If you could spend a day learning from anyone in the world, who would you choose?

I would have to say Denzel Washington. When I say that, people say, " Ah, you're just saying that because he's so fine." No! I'm not. When I read about him, he is just so down-to-earth, and he has interacted with so many people. I think he would share one-on-one. He seems to be very intelligent, very real, very well-read. I have so many heroes, people I could sit down with, like Harriet Tubman, Nelson Mandela. I know I can't have days with these people, but these are my heroes. There's also Michelle Obama. What I look for when I have a conversation with someone is the trading of information, a new idea, a new way of looking at something. If I grow a little bit during the conversation, those are the ones that I enjoy most.

I need to spend a day with someone who writes patterns. I also want to have conversations with people who are dyeing yarns because I never quite find the colors I want. Sometimes I fall in love with a yarn, and the next time I go to buy it, it's discontinued. You learn to make changes, but it's so much easier if I have to make repeats, and I know the yarn.

What direction do you see your business taking in the next few years?

I enjoy traveling, doing the vendor shows and the fashion shows, but I would like to do less of that.

I have a lot of clients come to me and ask, "Where is the pattern for this?" So I really want to learn how to make patterns. I'm not trying to hold onto information. I just don't know how to write a pattern yet. I'd like to start offering my patterns for sale and writing a book eventually.

I would keep it simple in the beginning. Even a beginner needs to understand that they can make a dress - that they can make a pantsuit. This is not magic. It can happen for you just like it's happened for me.

I enjoy what I do. I try to keep it fresh because I don't want to be bored. When new yarns come out, I'm as excited as a kid in a candy store because it gives me different opportunities: "Oh, I got something new to work with. Y'all watch out!"

This shawl draws upon the tools of our rigid heddle and certain yarn qualities to achieve the open, lacey effect of crochet.

I visualized how Mona Muhammad drapes her models in lots of sumptuous, lacey fabric when I created this piece.

Open Weave Shawl

I selected a variety of animal fibers with mohair in mind for its "grabby" nature. Finishing with hot water will bring out the fibers to retain an open but stable result.

I also focused on the textural variation created by using yarns of varying gauge. To get the wooly, super bulky yarn to keep from clinging to the adjacent ends while weaving, I use the strategy of placing these accents in holes to help them behave. We need an uneven number of ends in between to do this. We'll achieve that with focused, direct warping.

Finished Measurements approximately 13" (33 cm) W x 65" (162.5 cm) L

Equipment

- Rigid heddle loom with at least 16" (40.5 cm) of weaving width. Also see the notation for a 15" (38 cm) loom* p. 120.
- 5 dent reed
- 1 shuttle

Warp

"Thick and thin," super bulky wool yarn in a natural or ecru color. I tried handspun yarn from two sources at Etsy.com. I had more appealing results with what I call thick and thicker than with one that varied from very fine to bulky. Uses 39 yds. (36 m).

For a novelty texture (I refer to this as the lumpy novelty yarn), I used a fine gauge yarn with nubs, Lang Marlene, 70% cotton, 30% nylon. 50 gm = 153 yds (149 m). I warped this double-stranded** (closeup p. 110) since the nubs were far apart. I used 142 yds (130 m). Another good yarn for this is Tahki Ripple, 100% cotton, 50 gm = 142 yds (130 m). Single-stranded will use 71 yds (65 m). A sparkle yarn would be another attention-getter. Since there is lots of air space in this shawl, the cotton and wool combination doesn't seem to be a problem for differential shrinkage.

Warp and Weft

Fingering gauge, mohair or mohair blend. I used one skein of Green Mountain Spinnery Simply Fine in White 9212 (a natural shade), 40% kid mohair, 60% fine wool. 450 yds (412 m) per skein. Uses 255 yds (233.5 m).

Tip - Thick handspun yarn can be unpredictable. If the slubs start to loosen and stick in the reed, a little spray starch works quite well to keep it going.

5 epi, 4 - 5 ppi

Warp

15-3/4" (40 cm) W x 98" (249 cm) = 79 ends according to Diagrams A and B.

*For a narrower version on a 15" (38 cm) loom, perform the repeat 5 times rather than 6. The warp width will be 13-1/2" (34.5 cm) wide = 67 ends. The finished width will be approximately 11" (28 cm).

For direct warping, use Diagram A to put an odd number of ends between every super bulky strand. I want this thicker yarn to be in holes to control the movement of the yarn facilitate a clean shed.

If you are not familiar with my diagrams, these represent the reed with white heddles with holes and shaded areas for slots. The short vertical lines represent the yarn going into slots. Longer lines go into holes. If there is no vertical line, you skip that hole or slot. Pay attention here, and the rest is easy.

Key to the Diagrams: the numbers under the vertical lines are:

1 = 1 single strand of super bulky. Draw the end from the yarn ball into the hole, pull it to the peg, and tie it there. Then cut and tie that strand to the back apron rod at the loom.

2 = 1 loop of mohair fingering. You can carry this yarn across without cutting and tying off until the end.

3 = 1 loop of lumpy novelty yarn. Tie it on to the back apron rod, draw the loop, then cut and tie it off to the rod each time it appears.

**If you have a finer strand for #3 and want it to stand out more (see the closeup, p. 110), warping this double-strand is a little trickier but enhances the texture. The easiest way to do this is to place a loop where you come to #3 in the chart and a 2nd loop in the subsequent slot or hole. When you sley the reed, you only need to sley #2 as the double strands are already home.

Starting at the right of Diagram A below and facing the back of your loom, draw one single strand of super bulky as noted in the Key above. Proceeding left, you will draw 4 loops into slots, changing yarns as written until you draw the next single strand, #1. After this, you will draw 3 loops into holes, changing yarns as written. Complete the sequence under the green bar 4 times. End with the sequence at the left, noting that the last #2 at left is marked with a red *. This will be a single strand of #2 tied off at the peg.

Diagram A

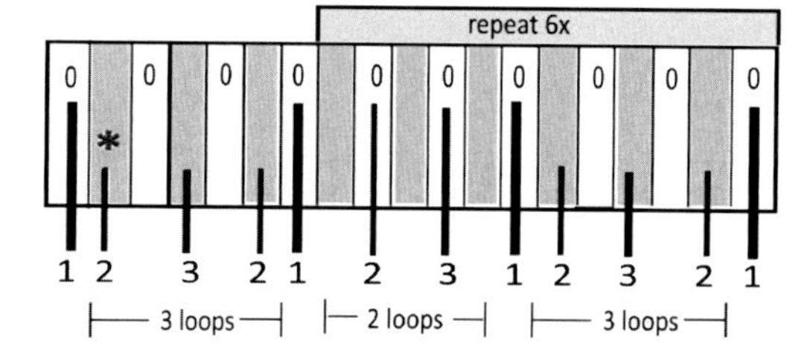

Diagram B is a visual of what happens when you sley the reed. It is the reverse of A because you are now facing the front of the loom.

Diagram B

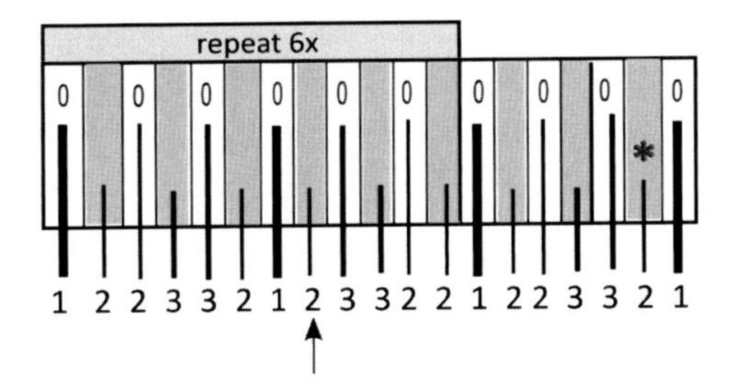

You only need to know three things here:

1. Sley to the empty slot or hole to the right.
2. At the left side of every other #1 strand, you will move one end from that slot to the slot on the other side of #1 (where marked with an arrow).
3. Leave each super bulky strand in its hole.

This puts 5 ends between every super bulky strand.

Weave

using the fingering gauge mohair according to the chart at right. Open plain weave refers to plain weave where the picks are carefully beat to about 1/4" (.5 cm) apart. You need that openness for the lace effect. The fabric will not be stable until after finishing, so handle the weft picks gently. Plain weave is given in inches/ cm, and Brooks Bouquet in the number of repeats.

Open Plain	Brooks Bouquet
6"(15 cm)	
	1 rep
28" (71 cm)	
	1 rep
2"(5 cm)	
	1 rep
28" (71 cm)	
	1 rep
6" (15 cm)	

Start your weaving up and from the right to make the modified Brooks Bouquet work as directed. Also, the weft will meander across where the slubs of the thick yarn catch it. Pull the selvages of the fabric outward to straighten the fell line and/ or use your finger to position weft where it catches. Otherwise, let it wander a bit. This shawl is all about variety rather than machine-straight lines.

Brooks Bouquet Modified to Highlight the Handspun

This variation places the super bulky yarn at strategic points of the "bouquets" and minimizes draw-in.

Starting from the right with the reed in the up position, wrap the shuttle around the 1st warp end to anchor it. Let the weft rise about 1/2" (1.5 cm) above the last pick. Pass the shuttle into the shed going under the first 6 ends. If you used any double strands, they count as one end. Exit the shed through the top (to the right of the 2nd strand of super bulky). *Go back 5 ends and re-enter the shed from the top. Pass the shuttle under those 5 plus 6 more ends before exiting the top (to the right of the 3rd strand of super bulky). You've surrounded 5 ends. Cinch that bundle tight. Repeat from *across. Try to keep the fell line straight and bundles cinched tightly as you work across. Surround the last 5 ends and exit left.

Change the shed, and throw a pick. Beat this pick to set it 1/2" (1.5 cm) above the last pick to complete 1 repeat.

Finish

Remove from the loom, tying 5 strand tassels with overhand knots at each end. Wash according to method three, p. 12, and trim fringe to desired length.

This shape is directly inspired by the KnottyLoop shrug on p. 116.

Getting woven fabric to form to shoulder curves poses more of a challenge than crocheted or knitted fabric. The problem was resolved with an angular set in sleeve.

Bell Sleeve Shrug

Subtle detailing in the flared sleeve with eyelet edge finish is featured in this simple shrug - a great way to add sleeves when you need a little extra layering.

The eyelet is created by cinching warp ends together with a Spanish lace weave. You'll weave front and back panels for three sections, machine stitching them together.

	Small	Medium	Large	X Large	2X
To Fit Bust Size	32-34"	36-38"	40-42"	44-46"	48-50"
	81.5-86.5 cm	91.5-96.5cm	101.6-106.5 cm	112-117 cm	122-127 cm

Equipment

- Loom with at least 14" (36 cm) weaving width
- 10 dent reed
- 1 shuttle
- Plastic hair pick or weft beater
- Sewing machine and coordinating thread
- Straight pins
- Painter's or masking tape to mark seams

Warp and Weft

6 (6, 7, 7, 7) balls Berroco Quinoa in Mushroom, 91% cotton, 9% nylon, 50 gm = 175 yds. Uses 1060 (1071, 1092, 1244, 1263) yds, 959.5 (980.5, 998.5, 1137.5, 1155) m.

Warp Accent Stripe

1 skein Berroco Modern Cotton DK in Sandy Point, 60% cotton, 40% viscose, 100 gm = 135 yds. Uses 79 (80, 81, 93, 95) yds, 72.5 (73, 74, 85, 87) m.

10 epi, 11 ppi

It is a good idea to keep track of how close your pieces are to the diagram measurements, p. 127, noting the seam allowances and how the shrug might fit your own body as you work. Compare the circumference just above the bustline, width at shoulders, and sleeve length to see if you need to adjust seam allowances and hems.

If you would like more ease under the arm or a longer yoke, you can add a couple of ends of Quinoa at the beginning and end of each warp.

You will warp 2 times as follows:

Warp Front & Back Yokes & Upper Arm Pieces

9-5/8" (24.5 cm) W x 110 (112, 116)", 280 (285, 295) cm L for sizes S, M, L = 96 ends

11" (28 cm) W x 118 (121)", 300 (308) cm for sizes XL, 2X = 110 ends

according to chart A below.

Chart A

	6x - S, M, L 7x - XL, 2X		
12		12	Quinoa
	2		Mod. Cotton

Weave Front & Back Yokes & Upper Arm Pieces

(make 6 pieces of different lengths) using Quinoa throughout. Cut and tuck weft tails at the end and beginning of each, separating them with 2 picks of scrap yarn.

Weave 2 at 19 (20, 21, 21-3/4, 22-1/2)", 48 (51, 53.5, 55.5, 57) cm L.

Weave 4 at 12 (12, 12-1/2, 12-1/2, 13)", 30.5 (30.5, 32, 32, 33) cm L.

Weave a footer and cut from the loom.

Warp Bell Sleeve Pieces

12-1/2" (32 cm) W x 94" (239 cm) L for sizes S, M, L = 124 ends

14" (35.5 cm) W x 94" (239 CM) for sizes XL, 2X = 140 ends

according to Chart B below.

Chart B

	8x - S, M, L 9x - XL, 2X		
12		12	Quinoa
	2		Mod. Cotton

IMPORTANT - When you sley the reed, make sure you sley from the slots to the hole to the right so that the right edge is in a hole. This will allow you to center the Spanish lace on each stripe as per directed.

Weave Sleeve Pieces

Start your weaving with the shuttle on the right with the heddle up for each piece. Using Quinoa throughout, weave 4 pieces, cutting and tucking weft tails in between and separating them with 2 picks of scrap yarn. Weave each piece the same as follows:

Weave 2" (5 cm) in plain weave.

Do one repeat of Spanish lace as follows: With the shuttle at the right, weave back and forth for 4 picks on only 7 raised ends. This will include the first end of the contrast stripe of Modern Cotton. Pull the weft tightly to draw that end in so that you are creating a hole. On the 5th pick, weave the next section between the next 2 ends of the contrast stripe with four picks. Use the hair pick or a weft beater to beat that section in place. You are including the 2nd end of the first contrast stripe when you weave to the right and the 1st end of the 2nd stripe when you weave to the left. Cinch those picks tightly.

After 4 picks, go on to the next section repeating across. Change the shed and throw the next pick all the way across to the right. You have created a small hole with a diagonal line in the middle, centered on the vertical stripe.

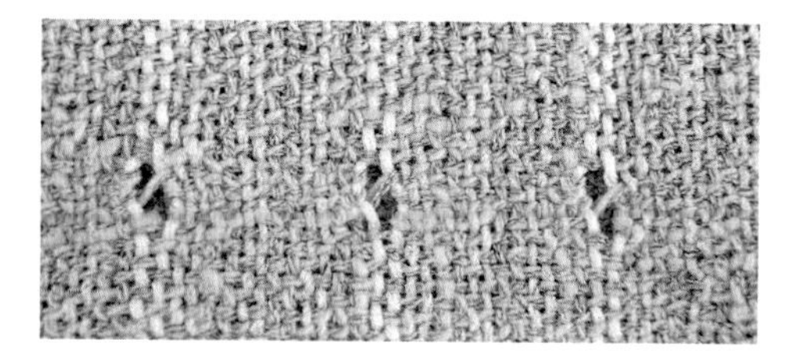

Finish with plain weave for a total length of 17-1/2" (44.5 cm).

Weave a footer and cut from the loom.

Finish

Raw finish each end before cutting apart, p. 18. Wash according to method one, p. 12.

Assemble - Detailed measurements of the finished piece are given in Diagram 2 on p. 127. Check the measurements before assembling. The shrug is reversible between front and back.

Gather the bell and connect the sleeve pieces: Stitch along one end of each of the 4 bell sleeve pieces by sewing 2 rows close together within 1/2" (1 cm) of the edge using a long stitch (4mm). Pull on the threads to gather evenly to match an end of each of the upper sleeve pieces. Pin the bell to the upper sleeve end, and sew with a 5/8" (1.5 cm) seam allowance. Don't worry about matching stripes here. Press the seam allowance toward the bell. Repeat for the other sleeve sections

Angled shoulder seam: With right sides together, pin an upper sleeve to a yoke piece. We will call this the front yoke. To sew this angled seam, mark 1-1/4" (3 cm) from the raw edge at one selvage with a pin and 1/4" (.5 cm) from the raw edge at the other selvage. Use masking or painter's tape to mark a straight line between those 2 points and sew close to the tape. See Diagram 1.

Note - the wide end of this seam is at the bottom edge of the yoke. Mark this edge with a pin.

Raw finish the seam allowance through all thicknesses close to the stitching, and trim to 1/4" (.5 cm).

Press the seam allowance toward the sleeve.

Sew the same angled seam on the other side of that yoke piece.

Important - Take the time to make sure that the wide portion of the angled seam is at the bottom edge of the yoke on each side so that the underarms converge, as shown in Diagram 2.

Complete the back yoke the same as the front.

Attach the front and back: with right sides together, sew with a skinny seam (2 picks) from the sleeve edge to the neck opening on each side per Diagram 2.

Sew the underarm seam with a skinny seam from the sleeve edge up to the underarm opening on each side.

Hem the sleeves: Turn and press a 1/2” (1.5 cm) hem along each sleeve and machine stitch. Sleeves are intended to hang about 1” (2.5 cm) from the knuckles of the hand. You may want to adjust this hem to your desired length.

Your shrug is ready to wear.

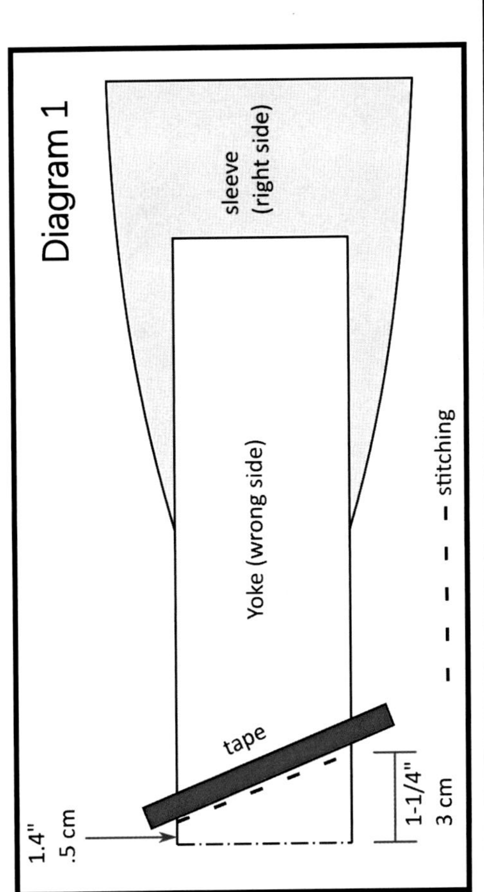

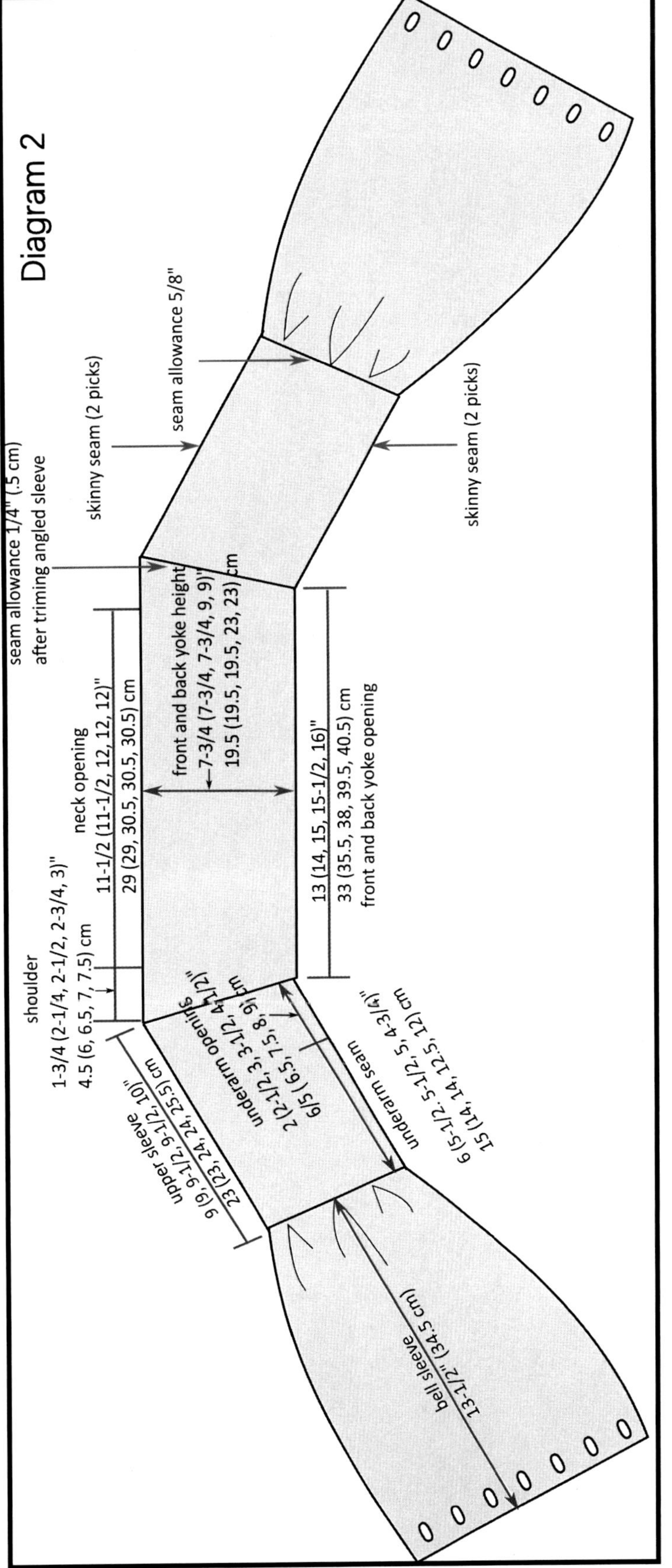

Chapter 7

"I strive for two things in design: simplicity and clarity. Great design is born of those two things."

- Lindo Leader

Keep it Simple

"Elegance is elimination."

- Cristóbal Balenciaga

German-born Dieter Rams was one of the most influential industrial designers of the 20th century. His understated, elegant approach continues to influence design today. In 1976, he presented his 10 principles for good design summarized as follows:

Good design:

1. is innovative.
2. makes a product useful.
3. is aesthetic.
4. makes a product understandable.
5. is unobtrusive.
6. is honest.
7. is long-lasting.
8. is thorough down to the last detail.
9. is environmentally friendly.
10. is as little design as possible.

Expanding on #10, he continues, "Less, but better - because it concentrates on the essential aspects, and the products are not burdened with non-essentials. Back to purity, back to simplicity."

These principles have influenced such greats as Steve Jobs, the design guru of Apple. In an interview with Business Week in 1998, Jobs stated, "That's been one of my mantras - focus and simplicity. Simple can be harder than complex: you have to work hard to get your thinking clean to make it simple. But it's worth it in the end because once you get there, you can move mountains."

Jobs' laserlike focus on the essential is also what made him highly productive. This chapter will examine the compelling nature of simple geometry and an updated approach to classic lines as inspired by the next artist, Lawrence Peters.

For the Urban Shawl, p. 136, I've employed a pared-down plaid. Plaid has a life of its own, from the tartans of Scottish clans to the luxury fashion house of Burberry of London. In the winter of 2020/21, animal prints make way for the sophistication of the square - a perfect time for weavers.

Along with plaid comes the pattern of the season - houndstooth. The tank top on p. 142 puts this simple pattern front and center.

And let's not forget, at the close of this unprecedented season, giving back to a community in need. On p. 166 in Chapter 9, I'll show weavers one way to play a part.

Lawrence Peters

Lawrence Peters is a transplant to my Tucson area. After many years in the East, he moved here from formative years in New York, Florida, and ultimately Massachusetts. When my neighbor introduced me to him, I was immediately inspired by his choice of pure color and simple geometry, which resonate with a quiet elegance in his work.

With a background in media sales for top home décor publications and his eye on fashion trends, Lawrence has carved out a business that took root in the East and transfers beautifully to the Southwest as both a weaver and an eco printer.

He is a veteran of the craft show circuit and is currently involved in gallery shows and the soon-to-be-launched *Red Front Door Store* online.

Under his business name, Bewoven Studio, find more about Lawrence and his work at

www.bewovenstudio.com.

I understand you left a 35-year career to take this leap into the fiber art world. What led you to move across the country as you did and to make that dramatic shift?

My career (i.e., media sales) ended - magazine ad revenues not being where they wanted them to be. The good thing is that I got to live in Florida (Winter Park). That was actually kind of fun, having lived so many years in Manhattan.

Then my partner and I decided I would move up to Massachusetts, where he was. Once I got up there, I had to figure out what to do with myself. I was pretty frantically looking for a job. In the midst of that, my mentor of many years said, "Why don't you take up the craft of weaving, since you always wanted to be a fashion designer?" I didn't know enough to say no!

So I took a class in rigid heddle. In my estimation, it did not go well. Either the instructor didn't know how to deal with people without any background or didn't care. I don't know, but the people in the class told me I should continue. Then a friend of mine from childhood who is a lifelong knitter told me I should check out the Harrisville Designs center. They had a 5-day intensive beginner class that was a terrific experience. The teacher, Tom Jipson, was very patient and didn't pressure me.

Looking back, it was pretty extraordinary - just the whole wonderful weaving community. All my classmates said, "You may not know it, but you really have something."

I bought an old loom at auction, the Schacht Baby Wolf that I still have today. I didn't know what I was buying at the time. Turns out, it was warped, and everything was a little out of skew. With the help of my cousin's husband, who is a wonderful woodworker, and a new beater race from Schacht, I was able to rebuild it.

I had heard the old line, "How do you learn how to weave - you have to weave a mile." I just kept

at it and kept at it. I had no concept that I would sell what I was weaving. Thankfully, there was a community of artisans to learn from, including a now-disbanded group, Artisans of WMass, which guided members through all the facets of craft sales. I have been so fortunate in connecting with people who are willing to share their knowledge and expertise.

When deciding where to retire, the Southwest was at the top of the list. We love western Massachusetts. It's gorgeous from spring to early winter, but the snow, the ice of winter, forget it. At first, we settled in Buckeye, Arizona, because an acquaintance lived nearby. I quickly became friends with a soap maker in our community who ran craft shows from her house, so I immediately had an artisan connection.

What are some of the lessons you learned about starting over?

I'm good at schmoozing. I'm always out looking for opportunities, but I really never, ever, ever want to do a start-up, outdoor craft show again. When I started doing shows, I had no idea how much physical labor went into setting up the booth.

Now that I'm older, it's just too much work and too dicey. I'm glad I did them for the experience.

You have to make sure that whatever your venue is, that it gets good foot traffic. I did a show that was well promoted, had a great branding, near Phoenix, but never really got the foot traffic as it was out in the middle of nowhere.

Also, I would have been more careful about the promotion. I did a free show at a gardening store in Scottsdale, which was appealing. As part of their plant sale, they have an artisan market, which they don't promote because they don't want it to interfere with selling their plants. I got to meet terrific fellow artisans, but people weren't there to buy art. They were there to buy plants.

Now I actually was selling well at the Phoenix Flea, a Modern Market. I thought of it as Phoenix's version of the Brooklyn Flea, meaning really cool stuff, hipsters, youngish crowd, stylish. Talk about what a great place to be. By my 3rd show, though, it was so longer working for me. I think that ultimately, the people there were not looking for art, or they were looking for a lower price point.

The market has been changing for shows. Some people have surmised that there is an over-saturation of art markets, pulling people in too many directions. I also think the bloom has been off the artisan market since the COVID thing.

I am in a gallery in Washington Depot in Connecticut. Also, my friend, Janna, the one who did craft shows from her house, moved to Flagstaff, and she's doing these porch sales. I'm now participating in that from a distance in that she has some of my inventory. Working with her and another person, we're creating our own online store from that and calling it *The Red Front Door Store.*

Your purse scarves - I have to admit this idea was not on my radar until I examined your work. What an excellent idea for weavers. How did you spot this trend, and what is your customer's response?

I was at the Phoenix Flea. A millennial came up to me and asked if I had thought about doing these little scarves that you could tie around your neck or put on your purse. I thought a lower price point would cannibalize my sales on a longer scarf, but I actually make a higher margin on these little pieces than I do on the bigger ones.

You have to have your spread of price points, affordable to high end. This way, they can see my work, and no one's going to balk at the price.

Eco printing is another technique you have added to your line. Can you briefly describe the process and what interests you in this direction?

Eco-printing is part of the natural dyeing tradition. Until we knew all about how to dye with chemicals, everything was pretty much naturally done. Indigo came from the Indigo plant, for example. You can use walnut shells. You can use madder root...

Rather than making a dye from the plant material, I am able to get the leaf or petal to

embed its color or pattern right into the silk. I took a workshop on eco-printing hosted by the weaving guild at Sun City West. The community has a vibrant activities center, and the weaving workshop is incredible.

What is it in the makeup of protein fiber that allows it to accept and hold on to dye from botanicals? I'm not a chemist, but it works. You can get them to work on cotton, but you have to open up those fibers chemically. The petals and the leaves must be in direct contact with the fabric, in my case, silk. You've got to get it tightly bound, and then you have to use pressure, heat, and moisture. To some extent, you're cooking it. Then you let it cure.

Sometimes you get unwanted surprises. I've printed with pomegranate leaves. They actually turned out beige. Eucalyptus can print an orangey-pink, a beige, or a green. I do think it depends on the time of the year. When most things are in bloom, in the height of spring, you seem to get a more intense color.

It's fun, and it's one of a kind. I don't know what is going to happen. There are techniques I've learned only through trial and error, and I've come up with some innovations that I think make my work unique. Some people rely on a lot of over -dying, and it works for them, but that's not what I want. I like things to be crisp, clean, and stand out.

I love the simple geometry of your weaving. What role does color play in your work?

In terms of the eco-dyeing, that's mother nature. I don't often mix a lot of botanicals together. I did a piece with various leaves from Flagstaff, which resulted in some blues, reds, and a little yellow. I don't know if I could ever reproduce it. That's the thing that's great.

When I weave, if we're talking about table runners, it's a combination of aesthetic and practicality. Similarly, with what I said about eco-printing, I like the patterning to be the star. I particularly like the huck pattern. I was drawn to the textured stripe pattern in *A Handweaver's Pattern Book* by Marguerite Porter Davison and made my own three stripe and four stripe drafts from it.

From the practical side, I thought that if I want something to shine, just focus on the pattern, and then I thought that most people have so much going on in their décor. They've got artwork, maybe oriental carpets, wallpaper, upholstery. Do they really want, on their table, yet another highly colorful piece of woven fabric that may clash with their china pattern?

So I decided that an elegant huck boxes table runner in natural, undyed, would go with anything. From there, I found some classic variations. I found a green that I really like. It's a version of the green that I had in my apartment back in Manhattan. Then there were other colors like an alabaster that I added that was a neutral but has a lot of different colors in it. I didn't want to be creating a line of 20 different colors. It's just me, and I didn't want to kill myself keeping up.

What are the people, places, or things that inspire your designs?

When I was in the magazine industry, I worked on publications like House Beautiful, Elle Décor, Metropolitan Home. I was exposed to Architectural Digest, House and Garden, and I lived in New York City, where clean, crisp design was always in vogue.

My inspiration was and still is home décor as well as the fashion magazines. I learned from JoAnn Barwick, who was, at one time the editor of House Beautiful, that readers relied on the editor, not only to spot trends but also for guidance.

I interacted with Margaret Russell, who was chief editor of Elle Décor and later Architectural Digest. I really had exposure to some top-line people, and living and working in Manhattan, I was surrounded by Madison Avenue, Bergdorf Goodman, Tiffany's. So I have my version of Calvin Klein in a weaving pattern.

I see from your Facebook posts that you have supported charitable work. What are your favorite causes, and how do you prefer to give back?

I've served on the world's largest AIDS service organization, called the AIDS Healthcare Foundation (AHF). I've been the treasurer, I've been on the finance committee, the grant fund committee. Part of the reason I did all that was that I was and always have been HIV negative. I felt that I should take my good health and use it to help other people.

The particular fundraiser on my Facebook page was for my birthday. I wanted to do something for the Native American community because they haven't been treated well by any stretch of the imagination. So I found First Nation on GuideStar Charity Navigator. They were one of the most highly rated nonprofits addressing Native American issues.

I've also donated woven and printed works to charitable auctions.

Editors Note: Inspired by Lawrence Peters' contributions, see p.166 for a pattern you can use to give back to your community.

Not your mother's shawl, the simple bright check and edge piece grant a pop of color to featherweight mohair.

Here's a unique method to create a V shape from a woven rectangle.

The Urban Shawl

The mohair and silk base give this shawl an elegant drape and translucence. I love the bloom of mohair yarn for an open weave. This fiber needs a lot of breathing room to weave easily. Plan a well-spaced warp and weft as given in the pattern. The fabric may be fragile until finishing in hot water to "shock" the yarn into stability.

You have two options here - knit the contrasting edge or weave it.

Approximate finished measurements: 80-84" (203-213.5 cm) W at top edge x 18-1/2" (47 cm) L

Equipment

- Rigid heddle loom with at least 17" (43 cm) weaving width
- 10 dent reed
- Painter's tape. You can use masking tape but remove some of the stickiness first by applying and removing it from scrap fabric (or your pant's leg as I do).
- Measuring tape or straight edge at least 44" (112 cm) long
- Sewing machine and coordinating thread
- Straight pins
- Tapestry needle and contrasting scrap yarn

Warp and Weft, Shawl Base, Version 1

2 skeins Hamilton Yarns Affeto Seta in Ebony and 1 skein in Rain Cloud, 70% kid mohair, 30% silk, 50 gm = 262 yds (240 m). Uses 441 yds (403.5 m) of Ebony and 72 yds (66 m) of Rain Cloud.

Affeto Seta is unique in its texture and gauge. It has a short fiber without a lot of mohair's fuzziness, but all of the sheen, which makes it weave beautifully. If using traditional brushed mohair, you may want to use an 8 dent reed for more room for the longer fiber. In this case, reduce the repeat of the striping to 5 times for a 17-1/2" wide warp giving you a slightly deeper shawl.

Warp and Weft, Shawl Edge, Version 1

I used Berroco Quinoa in Blueberry for the main color, 91% pima cotton, 9% modal, 50 gm = 175 yds (160 m) Uses 140 yds (128 m) - 1 ball. It appears that Berroco may have discontinued that color, although there are still a few balls of it out there. Admittedly the nubby texture of this yarn made sewing it onto the mohair a challenge. A good substitute that will be easier to sew is one skein of Berroco Modern Cotton DK, 60% pima cotton, 40% nylon, 100 gm = 209 yds (191 m).

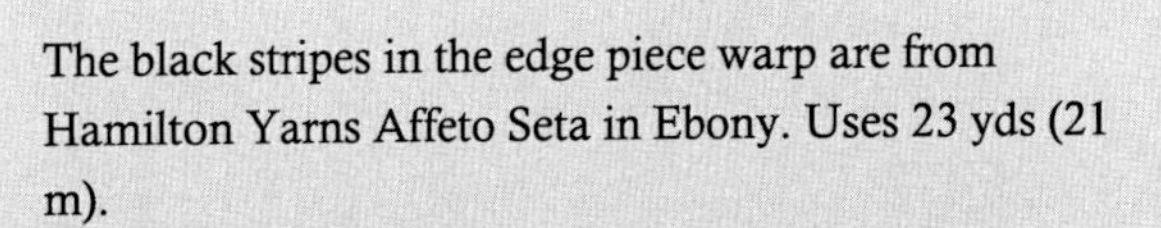
The black stripes in the edge piece warp are from Hamilton Yarns Affeto Seta in Ebony. Uses 23 yds (21 m).

For Yarns used in Version 2, Knitted Edge, see p. 141.

10 epi, 8-9 ppi

Version 1, Woven Edge

You will warp twice for this version.

Warp the Base

16-1/2" (42 cm) W x 66" (167.5 cm) L (164 ends) according to the chart below. See chart reading p. 10.

	6x		
20		20	Black
	4		Contrast

Weave the Base

repeating the sequence in the weaving chart below until the piece measures approximately 40", ending with the main color, black. Pay attention to keep your weft spacing no closer than 8-9 ppi to achieve the airiness intended. See the photo below. The fabric will be somewhat fragile (weft can shift if tested) until wet finishing.

Contrast	Black
	20
4	

Weave a 1/2" footer, cut the weaving from the loom, and continue on to complete the edge piece.

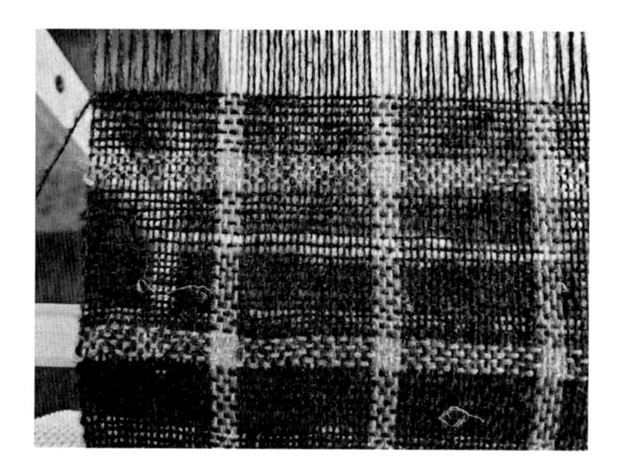

Warp the Edge Piece

4-1/2" (11.5 cm) W x 126" (320 cm) L = 46 ends, according to the chart below.

		2x			
8		2		28	Main
	2		2		Black

Weave the Edge Piece

10 epi, 11 ppi

for 102" (259 cm) using the Main color. Weave a 1/2" (1.5 cm) footer and cut the weaving from the loom.

Finish

Raw finish each edge, p. 18. Wash the body piece according to method three and the edge piece according to method one on p. 12.

Form the Triangles

You can use this method whenever you want to split a rectangle with a straight line. With a straight edge or metal tape measure, lay the edge from one corner point to the other. Place painter's tape along that edge (Figure 1). Remove the straight edge. Using the tapestry needle and scrap yarn, hand sew a running stitch along the designated edge (Figure 2). Tie a knot in the scrap yarn at each end of the stitching so it doesn't slip during the next step.

We will machine stitch 3 times on each side along the diagonal for a very secure edge. First, sew about 1/8" (3 mm) away from each side of your yarn marking. Use a straight stitch and go slowly to avoid catching the scrap yarn. This marks the line that you will avoid crossing. Now double zigzag the outer edge of each straight line you just stitched.

Cut along the yarn marking to separate the 2 pieces.

Center Back seam: Pin the triangles together at the center back (see the diagram on the next page), matching the stripes as on p. 18. Sew with a 1/2" (1.5 cm) seam allowance. Press the seam open.

Attach the Edge Piece: center the edge piece selvage that is farthest from the stripes along the triangle's long side. Place that piece on top, overlapping by 1/2" (1.5 cm). You should have about 7" (18 cm) of the edge piece extending beyond both sides.

Pin the pieces together carefully as the overlap seam can shift easily. I use lots of pins parallel to the sewing line and remove them as I stitch. Sew close to the selvage of the edge piece, then sew 1/4" (.5) cm away.

Bevel the Edge Piece: Use the painter's tape to mark a line from where the triangle attaches to the body up to the outer corner of the edge piece. The angle may be slightly different than established by the triangle.

Figure 1

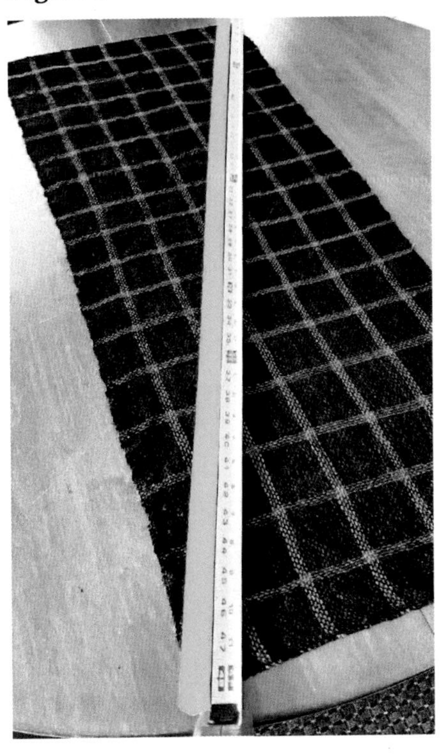

Figure 2

Here's one for the knitters.

Complete the shawl triangle according to Version 1. Rather than weaving the edge piece, you'll pick up along the long edge with the knitting instructions that follow.

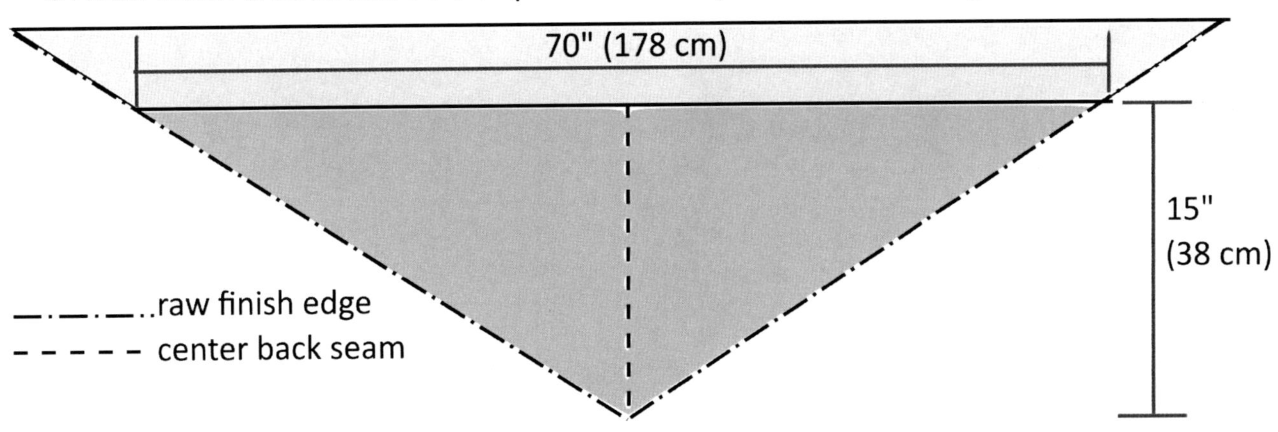

With matching thread, raw finish the edge piece with the tape as your guide, and trim neatly.

Check the endpoints where the triangle attaches to the edge piece. You may need to use the tapestry needle to weave in a supplementary mohair strand to neaten and secure these connections.

Version 2, Knitted Edge

Follow the instructions on p. 138 to weave and assemble the triangle base of the shawl. It is important to wash this according to method three on p. 12 before proceeding.

Knitted edge: Gauge is approximately 17 sts = 4" (10 cm) in garter stitch (knit all rows).

Warp and Weft used

2 skeins of Hamilton Yarns Affeto Seta and 72 yds of Diamond Yarn Pure Superkid Mohair in Rust #1525. 100% mohair, 50 gm = 226 yds (207 m).

Diamond Pure Superkid Mohair is an excellent match to Affeto Seta. I can't recommend using it for the main color, however. It reacts in an unusual way to static electricity in my dry climate that makes it difficult to weave with if using overall.

You will need US 5 (3.75 mm), 40" (100 cm) circular knitting needles, and 1 skein of Noro Sonata in color 10, Chestnut. 35% cotton, 25% rayon, 20% silk, 20% nylon, 100 gm = 394 yds (360 m). Uses 270 yds.

Pick up 330 sts over the long edge on the front with Noro Sonata. This might seem like a lot of stitches, but it will go fast if you mark off 4" (10 cm) increments with locking stitch markers and shoot for 17 stitches over 4" (10 cm). If you are off by a couple of stitches, that's fine.

The shawl points will be a little fragile, so handle the crochet hook carefully at each end and start picking up stitches a couple of picks away from these points. You can reinforce the gaps here later.

I use a crochet hook without a handle to pick up the 17 stitches and then offload them from the opposite end onto the needles.

With garter stitch throughout, work 22 rows in Sonata, increasing at each end of every front side row by knitting in front and back of the stitch. Then *knit 2 rows of Ebony Affeto Seta, 2 rows of Sonata. Repeat from * two more times, continuing the increases at each end on all front side rows.

End with 2 more rows of Sonata with the front side increase, and bind off loosely.

With houndstooth emerging in fashion this year, I was inspired to design this summer-into-winter tank top.

Houndstooth Tank

Houndstooth weave is one of our easiest patterns to create and so style worthy.

Bamboo, cotton, and rayon give this fabric the necessary drape, breathability, and washability for wearing next to the body or in layers. Angling the underarm sections allows a subtle flare at the hip.

This one has 0-2" (0-5 cm) of ease. For a simple yet stylish accent, try the houndstooth pattern in a coordinating scarf.

Finished Measurements: See Diagram p. 147.

	Small	**Medium**	**Large**
To fit bust	32-34"	36-38"	40-42"
	81.5-86.5 cm	91.5-96.5 cm	112-117 cm
Measurement at bust	34"	38"	42"
	86.5 cm	96.5 cm	117 cm

Equipment

- Loom with at least 9" (23 cm) weaving width
- 10 dent reed
- 2 shuttles
- Sewing machine and coordinating thread
- Painter's or masking tape to mark angled seams
- 2-1/2 yds (2.25 m) of 3/4" (2cm) wide black lace seam binding

Warp and Weft

2 balls Universal Yarn Bamboo Pop in Sage, 50% bamboo, 50% cotton, 100 gm = 291 yds (266 gm). Uses 484 (518, 553) yds, 443 (474, 506) m.

1 skein Interlacements ZigZag in Black, 100% rayon, 8 oz. = 500 yds (457 m). Uses 177 (205, 234) yds, 162 (187.5, 214) m.

10 epi, 9-10 ppi. You will warp twice.

Diagram 3 on p. 147 shows you the approximate finished measurements for each size. Check your measurements before you start and while assembling for adjustments as needed. I prefer mine with 0" of ease. Reducing the houndstooth warp by 4 ends results in a 2" (5 cm) reduction around the bustline.

Warp the Houndstooth Panels

7-3/4 (8-3/4, 10)", 19.5 (22, 25.5) cm W x 95 (96, 96)", 241.5 (244, 244) cm L 76 (88, 100) ends. alternating one loop of Bamboo Pop with one loop of ZigZag across.

Sley the reed normally. This alternates 2 ends of Bamboo Pop and 2 ends of ZigZag across.

Weave the Houndstooth Panels **(make 4 pieces of different lengths)**

Wind one shuttle with ZigZag and one with Bamboo Pop. Weave, alternating 2 picks of each throughout. See "Alternating 2 Weft Colors" on the next page. To separate the pieces, weave 2 picks of contrasting scrap yarn between each, cutting and tucking all ending and beginning tails.

Make 2 pieces 14-1/2 (37 cm) long for all sizes.

Weave one front panel 18-1/2 (19, 19)", 47 (48.5, 48.5) cm long

Weave one back panel 23 (23-1/2, 24)", 58.5 (59.5, 61) cm long.

Weave a 1/2" (1.5 cm) footer and cut from the loom.

Warp the Shoulder Straps

5" (12.5 cm) W x 120 (122, 124)", 305 (310, 315) cm L (48 ends) with Bamboo Pop.

Weave the Shoulder Straps **(make 4)**

with Bamboo Pop for 24 (24-1/2, 25)" 61 (62, 63.5) cm. Make 4 equal pieces cutting and tucking ending and beginning tails and separating each with 2 picks of contrasting scrap yarn.

Weave a 1/2" (1.5 cm) footer and cut from the loom.

Finish

Raw finish all ends, p. 18. Wash according to method one, p. 12.

Assemble

Once you begin to piece this together, take the time to make sure you keep right and wrong sides and top and bottom edges identified (as applicable).

Front and Back Center Panels: Hem each of these 2 panels to finish the neck opening by overlapping the lace seam binding 1/2" (1.5 cm) along the right side of the top edge. Pin in place and sew together along the seam binding edge. Turn this edge to the inside and press for hemming. There should be just 2 picks showing beyond the seam binding at the edge. On the outside, stitch 5/8" (1.6 cm) from the edge.

With right sides together, pin one side of the front panel to a shoulder strap piece, matching the bottom edges. Sew together with a 1/2" (1.5 cm) allowance. Repeat on the other side of the front panel. Add the strap pieces to the back panel in the same way.

Alternating 2 Weft Colors

When your 2 shuttles are on the same side, you might wonder how these yarns should wrap around each other as you continue.

Below, I show what I call the **"Under/Under - Over/Over"** technique. If the weft from the last pick thrown is sitting under the outermost warp thread, you take the next shuttle and wrap it under the previous shuttle thread before throwing. If the weft from the last pick thrown is sitting over the outermost warp thread, the next shuttle wraps its thread over the thread of the previous shuttle before throwing. This keeps the yarn from sinking into the shed and missing the outermost warp end. Once you get the hang of this, you can think less about your edge and weave more quickly.

Diagram 1

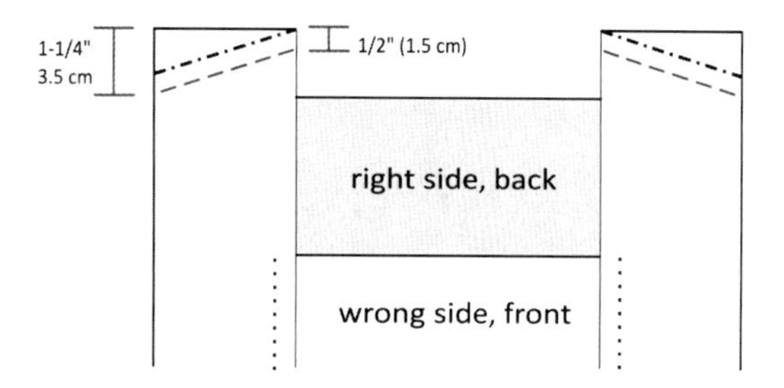

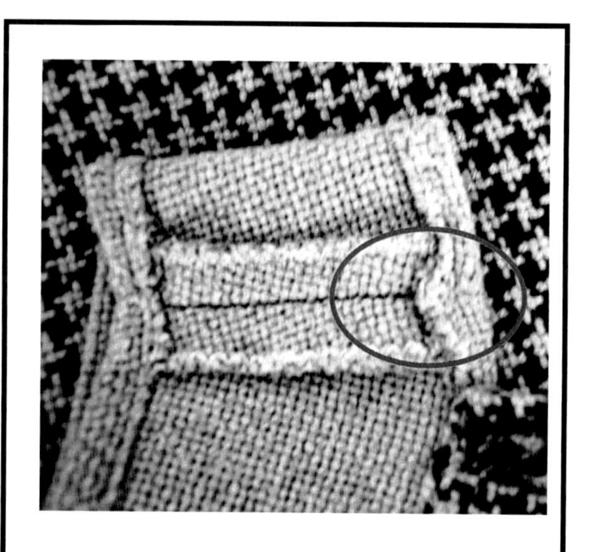

Shoulder seams: With right sides together, pin shoulder straps together at the top. Mark 1-1/4" (3.5 cm) from the top outer edge of the straps with a pin and 1/2" (1.5 cm) on the inside edge. Sew a straight line between the two points as shown in Diagram 1 above. You can place tape at the edge of each mark to guide your stitching, but I usually just "eyeball" the straight line for short seams.

Raw finish the front and back layers of the shoulder seam to a 1/2" (1.5 cm) allowance to press the seams open. Press the center seams toward the strap, folding them over the shoulder seams. There will be a point formed on the fold as you ease stitch around the inner shoulder curve as circled in the photo at top right.

On the outside of the shoulder straps, topstitch the inner side 1/4" (.5 cm) away from the edge through all thicknesses. Sew from the bottom edge of the front, pivoting at the shoulder, to the bottom edge of the back.

Shape the underarm panels:

Mark two points at one end of the underarm panels that are 3/4" (2 cm) inward from each selvage. Place painter's or masking tape close to the bottom corners and up to border the marked points as a sewing guide (Diagram 2). Raw finish

Diagram 2

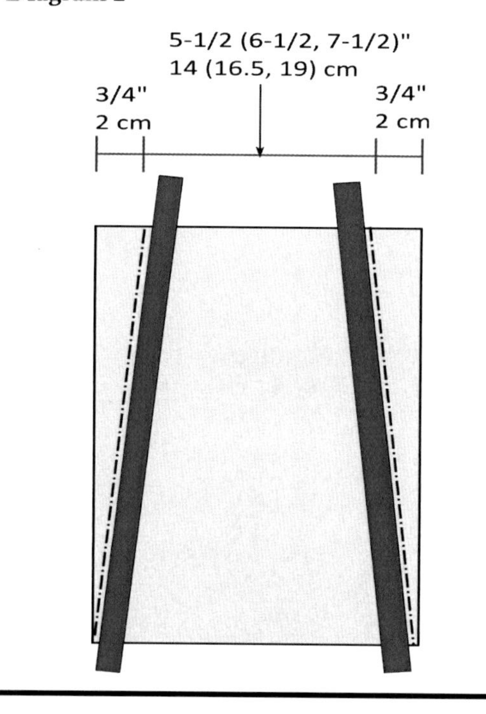

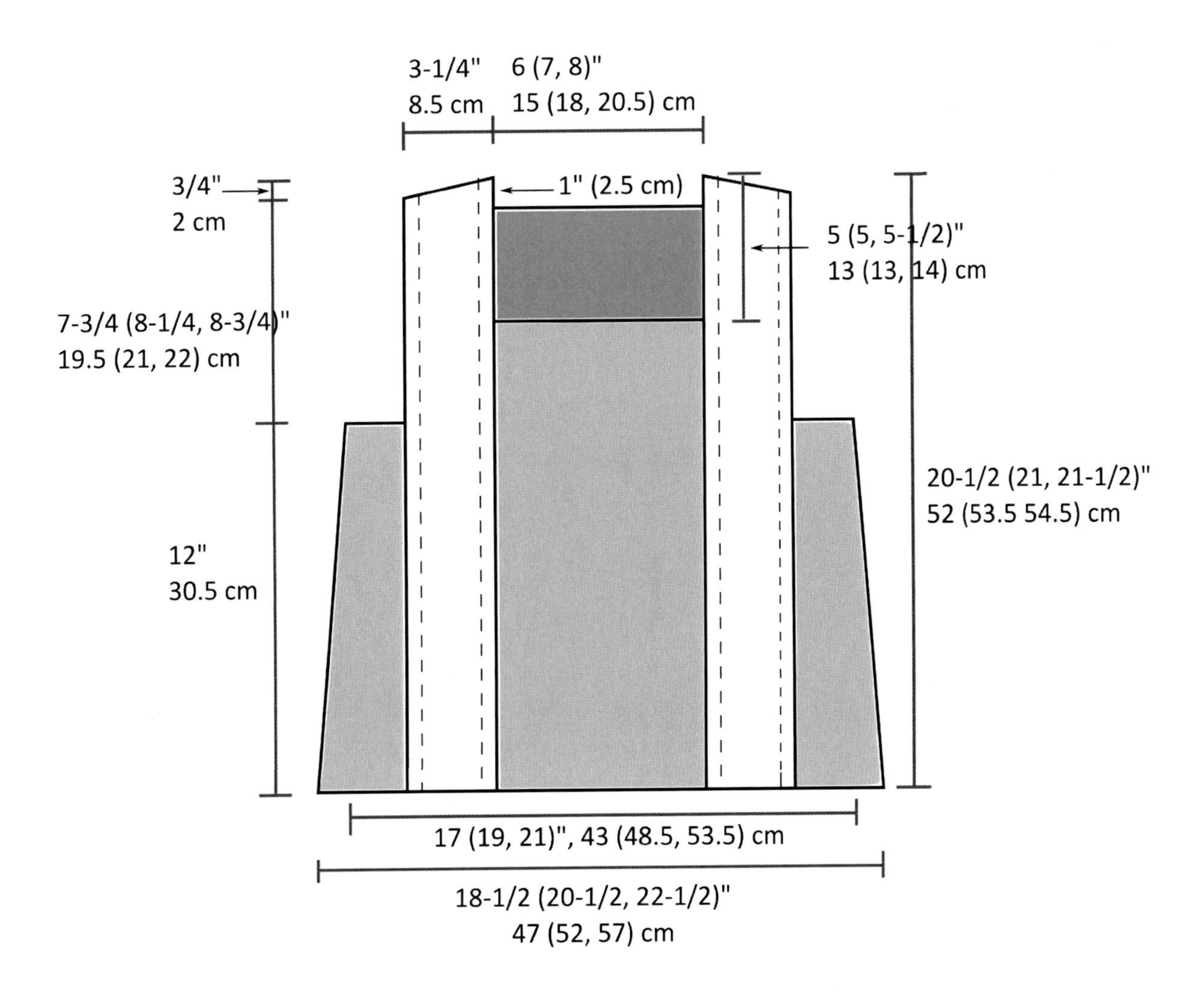

along the diagonal tape guide, p. 18. Remove the tape, and trim close to the finished edge.

Hem the narrow edge of the underarm panels with the lace seam binding as you did for the front and back panels, p. 144.

Attach the underarm panels to the straps: With the narrow (hemmed) side of the underarm panel up, pin and sew this piece to the front shoulder strap lining it up with the bottom of the strap, right sides together. Attach the panel to the back strap in the same way.

Press the seam allowances toward the strap, and topstitch 1/4" away from the strap edge on the right side, sewing from the bottom front edge to the bottom back edge, and pivoting at the shoulder seam.

Attach the other underarm panel to the other side, press, and topstitch. I opened up the free arm on my sewing machine to make this easier.

Complete the bottom hem with lace seam binding. Turn and press it to the inside, and sew (on the right side) around the bottom, 5/8" (1.6 cm) from the edge.

Your top is ready to wear.

Chapter 8

Reuse and Renew

"If the artist has outer and inner eyes for nature, nature rewards him by giving him inspiration."

-Wassily Kandinsky

"The artist is a receptacle for emotions that come from all over the place: from the sky, from the earth, from a scrap of paper, from a passing shape, from a spider's web."

-Pablo Picasso

Wikipedia defines upcycling, also known as creative reuse, as the process of transforming by-products, waste materials, useless or unwanted products into new materials or products of better quality and environmental value.

I remember a certain science professor in my college days who proclaimed that, at the current rate we were polluting our planet, there would be no trees left in Washington DC in 25 years. For me, that was a pivotal moment that sparked a profound concern for preserving our world.

That was over four decades ago. If we presume this teacher's statement was correct at that time, then we can credit the activists and participants who have worked hard to slow that contamination. As crafters, we can do our part.

Bringing new ideas to life is what enriches us, but do these things always serve their intended purpose? Do we put them to good use? If not, sell, donate, or consider upcycling.

The wall hanging on p. 76 took something that was living in one of my drawers and turned it into something that graces my wall and makes me happy whenever I pass by it.

My *Man Purse* on p. 28 is another piece put to use toward the same end.

Also, don't forget that we can choose yarns from recycled and sustainable fibers that we can feel good about, like the baby blankets on p. 166.

My next artist was creating beautiful things from cast-offs long before upcycling was a top-of-mind subject. Sue Burns has produced must-have, stylish, and original designs from used woolens for almost three decades.

I took particular interest in her description of how she has used random influence to change the course of her life and her design. The story of finding her place as she promotes eco-consciousness is a fascinating one as you read onward.

Sue Burns & Baabaazuzu

If you are on a discovery tour along the beautiful northern-most regions of Michigan's lower peninsula, you will want to find Baabaazuzu in the village of Lake Leelanau. This shop and showroom are where Sue and Kevin Burns and their team create one-of-a-kind wearable masterpieces from once-loved, repurposed woolens. Leelanau, meaning "delight of life," was the name that early Native Americans gave the lake and is the perfect backdrop for this "Michigan Made" brand.

Working in concert, the Burnses have successfully grown from a cottage industry to distribution through nearly 600 retailers in the US, Canada, Japan, and South Korea. Their line of sweaters, scarves, hats, bags, and signature mittens and fingerless gloves is designed for both men and women.

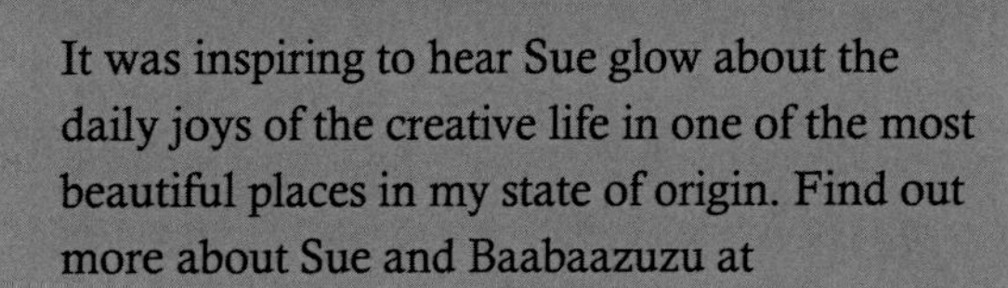

It was inspiring to hear Sue glow about the daily joys of the creative life in one of the most beautiful places in my state of origin. Find out more about Sue and Baabaazuzu at

www.baabaazuzu.com.

I love your business name. Where does the name Baabaazuzu come from?

I like to say, "I'm the Zuzu of Baabaazuzu" because that's my nickname for Sue, and then Baabaa is for the wool. It all rolls together pretty nicely, gets a little rhythm as you say it. People like it and are curious about it, so it always ends up in a conversation because nothing else sounds remotely like it.

I read that you have been designing since 1993. The accident that led to your work is a great story. For our readers, tell us how you got into garment design and specifically upcycling?

We debuted as a children's line due to a laundry error. That was my husband being helpful when he mistakenly put my favorite wool sweaters into the dryer. We had a three and a six-year-old at that time. I grew up literally behind a sewing machine - took sewing all the way through high school as some of us did back then - my mother made my clothes. With that experience and my background in graphic design, I went into salvaging that little bit of carnage into wearables for our then young daughters.

I made them a cute little coat, matching hat. We all know that when sweaters shrink, they look like they might fit a little kid, but they are not quite right. I started to think I would shorten the sleeves, but then I got to thinking, "Well, that sleeve doesn't have to go back on that same sweater…" That's how I got into the different combinations of patterns and colors.

So I sent my daughters out the door, thinking nothing of it. People were stopping me, asking where did I get these pieces. That was my lightbulb moment.

In my first year marketing a children's line, I had so many women clamoring for the same look, I had to answer that call, but now it was like, "How am I going to supersize something I'm shrinking?"

So I started with a simple women's vest, no sleeves, no collar, and it just grew from there. We figured out how to add the components for our jacket and so on. The fall away from that was useful fabric. That's how we created our mittens and lots of things down the line.

What challenges have you faced in growing your business?

When we started 27 years ago, there wasn't anyone that looked like us - not a single pair of recycled mittens or anything. When we went to our first wholesale buyer's market, we were so proud of

what we had to bring and our story. Retail buyers would come into our booth because they liked our look.

Then, as they were backing out of the booth, they were saying, "I don't think my customer wants used clothing!" So it was an uphill battle in the beginning.

Seven years into our initiative, people were doing cartwheels. It was, "Sign me up, double my orders." It was interesting to watch the mindset change. We had a pretty good 10-year dance being the only ones out there doing what we do, but it inspired a lot of look-alikes later that became another problem. One thing that sets us apart that we've always adhered to is our focus on quality, construction, and our combination of color and texture. We continue to innovate. I feel like we are unrivaled in all of those areas, and we have to be. I have to be able to sleep at night, knowing that what I send out the door doesn't end back on our doorstep.

Also, finding out where we fit in as a brand has been a challenge. The bulk of our business is still selling to stores. Some say we're too handcrafted if we're in a gallery or museum store. Other avenues like fine craft stores sometimes say we look too manufactured.

I see that you taught your husband to sew with you. What is the breakdown of roles that each of you plays in your business?

When I first started, it was just me. As the business was growing, I realized I had to enlist someone. We had just sold a restaurant and didn't know where we were going. I figured, "Who better than Kevin?" He could already cook. If he can cook, he can sew, right?

In the very beginning, we used a little Sears Kenmore, which he quickly burned out. Then I got him a nice, big, manly industrial machine. He was really adept at it.

We've always been a good team - we ran the restaurant together. In the restaurant, as in this business, we had our roles carved out in the beginning. In any business, though, there are more than just two hats to wear. Along the way, we fell into our other roles.

Here I create and design. I have one other gal that works alongside me. Kevin does all the prep work, and he is still the shrinker! He shrinks all day long (processes our raw goods in our intense felting process), and then he does the breakdown. All of our products use different types of wool, which are post-consumer garments that do different things in our process. We couldn't possibly use our thickest types of wool for a scarf, for example. It just wouldn't hang or drape properly. We've learned how to use everything because that's our mission: to save all of these things from the landfill. Besides that, we do pay for these things, so we've learned to use everything from the lightest to the heaviest.

One of the things we've taken into consideration is the firmness of the edges. Some of our products have a raw edge, and some of the wools we get simply won't do that. Since we get a lot of these, we've had to create products with no raw edges as well. Everything we get is inspirational, every color or cable. In my heart, I want to use it all because I think it's all beautiful.

Kevin starts that process. He knows what those qualities are that we are looking for, dissects each garment for us, and separates and labels them into what they will become. He also does a lot of the finance, paperwork, and shipping - things that free me up to keep the creativity going.

I also do the customer service. Sometimes it's a matter of who is available. We're just a good team that way.

What are your most important considerations and influences when you approach a new design?

Looking at trends and listening to my customers are my biggest inspirations. Let's go back to maybe 12 years ago - fingerless gloves. I'm now known for the warmest mittens in the world, and I have people coming to me for fingerless gloves. Why in the world would I make fingerless gloves? I'm about keeping people warm. I heard everything from texting to smoking. Then one mother in Chicago made sense to me when she said, "I love your mittens, but I have to take them off to do the buckle on the baby seat" and all that.

So I made fingerless gloves, and they are our biggest seller, alongside our mittens.

Another big suggestion from our customers - men. "How come you don't make anything for men?" So now we have a men's line.

Sometimes we just open our bale of wool. The pieces fly and fall on top of each other, and we say, "Wow, look at the combination there." Sometimes one sweater will inspire a design. It's a matter of keeping your eyes wide open. I don't need to sleep. I'm always looking for the next step.

What are some of the best places to source materials for upcycling?

The obvious would be a Goodwill or a second-hand store in your community. It's a great way to support those outlets right in your back yard that are doing good things.

I always think it can start in your own closet too. We have lots of people that bring to us their own personal wool items that are no longer useful in their current form, but they are in some way dear, and they can't part with them.

Take a look in your closet. It could be a sweater or a pair of jeans that don't fit right anymore, but

you just can't get rid of them. Repurpose it into something you would use every day.

What do you consider your greatest success in your 27 years in business?

I think our greatest success is that we have built so many long term relationships with our customers, from our wholesale stores (some of whom we have been with for 20 years) to our direct-to-consumer customers. These relationships are so heartfelt to me. That's part of what fuels me every day besides being immersed in all of this creativity. It's the fact that someone every day says, "I love what you do."

... and your biggest disappointments?

We tried some things that didn't pan out. We have been an all fall/winter line, and we tried some things to be a spring/summer. Looking back, I would call these efforts painful to put as much effort as we did into that because it didn't achieve the other entity's success.

We did some things with all new-fabric that just didn't resonate with me, and it didn't resonate with my customers either. It just wasn't Baabaazuzu enough. I also tried recycled kimono. Wool is very different. It wears so long. I just couldn't find the same qualities in other fabrics.

I am happy to have that behind me, but I'm glad I did all that because I would still wonder if I should.

What goals have you set for your work or your business going forward?

We write a lot of our orders at wholesale gift shows with handcrafted, made-in-America participants. We've seen, even pre-COVID-19, a dramatic buyer drop-off. We can guess that's because there are a lot less brick and mortar stores with Etsy and Amazon and so on.

So one of our challenges is staying relevant to what's new. We have an Etsy store, and we sell on Amazon. All of our things are one-of-a-kind, so it can be difficult for us to fit into some kind of sales platform. Amazon has a handmade section, so you get what you see in the photo. Our website works somewhat like that with a one-of-a-kind page. Then we sell in what I would say is a generic section where we have a dropdown with seven colorways that we can reliably repeat. If you ordered mittens, you might not get the pair in the photo, but it would be in that colorway. So we make it work.

The bridge to our customer is changing, and we can't ignore those outlets. At the same time, I continue to nurture my wholesale relationships. Our goal is to get a little bit of Baabaazuzu onto every head and hand.

Too Many scarves? Here's how I found new life for the extras in my collection.

Upcycled Scarves Tunic

Celebrate asymmetry in this multi-color, multi-texture tunic, loosely constructed for 4-6" (10-15 cm) of ease.

The idea is to use scarves that may be idle in your closet, but If you don't have enough scarves that work, I have reprinted the pattern for my confetti scarves for the outer pieces (done in two color schemes), p. 160. This pattern was originally published in the Schacht Spindle Co. blog, April 2019, and has been updated for tunic sizes.

I cut my center pieces from another unused scarf, but I've prepared a custom scarf pattern for those center pieces if you are starting from scratch, p. 162.

Equipment and Materials

- 3 scarves of coordinating colors, Approximate length and widths are suggested for your size on p. 158.
- Sewing machine, straight pins, and coordinating thread to assemble
- Painter's or masking tape to mark the shoulder slant

Making It Work

The diagram at right shows the approximate finished dimensions (after seaming the panels and hemming at the neck opening) for S (M, L, XL).

The tunic hangs 27" (68.5 cm) from the shoulder at the neck edge for all sizes. If your scarves are 54" or longer, you can tailor the length by unraveling per the instructions that follow. The center scarf should be around 5-1/2" (14 cm) wide for all sizes before seaming. The minimum finished width of the scarves (before seaming) for each size are:

Small 32"-34"

2 outer pieces = 7-1/4" (18.5 cm)

Medium 36" - 38"

2 outer pieces = 8-1/4" (21 cm)

Large, bust size 40" - 42"

2 outer pieces = 9-1/4" (23.5 cm)

X Large, bust size 44-48"

2 outer pieces = 10-1/4" (26 cm)

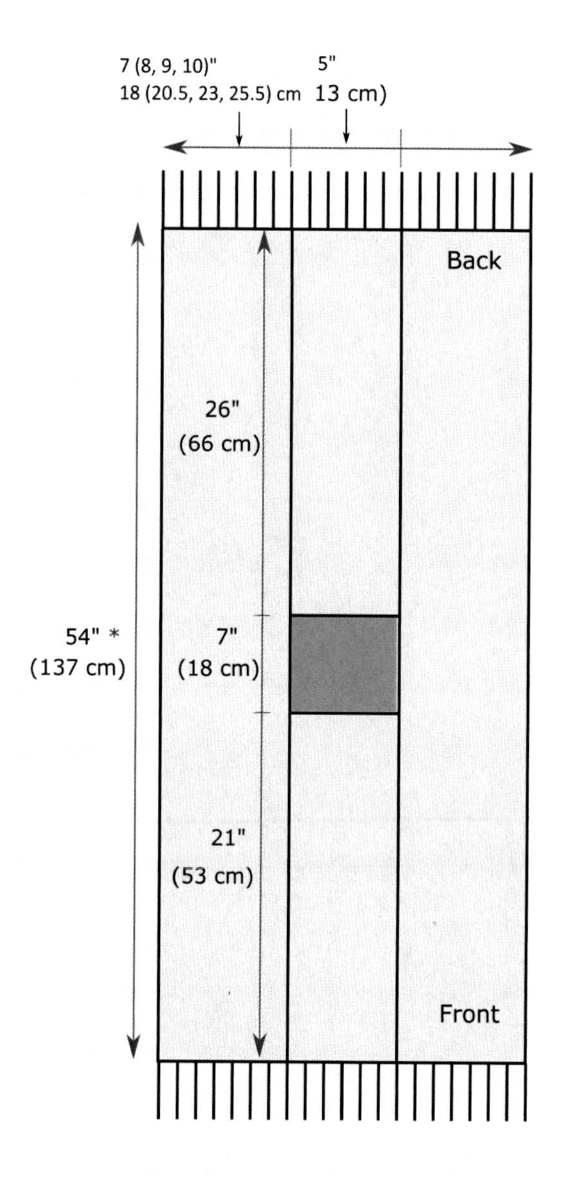

* Tunic hangs 27" from the shoulder at the neck opening (not including fringe) in this example.

These are only suggested sizes. What you have on hand may vary. There is lots of room to improvise here. Example: One of my outer scarves was slightly wider than the other, yet no one seems to notice due to the asymmetry.

Also, I had to unravel to shorten one of the outer scarves several inches.

The easiest way to unravel is to use the method shown in my YouTube video, "A Simple Method to Remove Weaving from the Rigid Heddle Loom" This involves cutting the weft up the middle to the place where you want to stop unraveling. Tape the piece to a table and cut the weft to the unraveling point. To ensure that you cut only weft, use a small, sharp pair of scissors. For each cut, tilt the bottom blade of the scissors upward so that the tip pokes out above the fabric. This way, only horizontal threads are sitting on the blade when you cut.

Then, starting on one side, grab the bottom strand about an inch inward from the edge, and you can pull the cut weft strands out two at a time. Retie the fringe, then remove the weft from the other side, and finish tying across.

Assemble

Prepare the center panels: Your scarves should be washed and dried before assembling.

Mark the back length of 27" (68.5 cm) above one fringed edge. This is the finished length plus a 1" (2.5 cm) hem at the neck. One way to mark it is to take a tapestry needle and sew a contrasting scrap thread from selvage to selvage. Raw finish (p. 18) on both sides of the scrap marker, finishing the other piece at approximately 22" (56 cm). Cut close to the raw finish edges.

Fold the cut edges to the wrong side, adjusting the hems to obtain the lengths in the diagram, and press. Be careful to use a pressing cloth if you have synthetic yarns in your fabric. Also, take the time to make sure the hem fold has the same length on both edges so it hangs level. before sewing 1/2" (1.5 cm) from the fold.

You may need to angle the hems to get the neck opening to hang straight. It is not uncommon for our rectangles to have one selvage longer than another.

Attach the panels: Pin the front center panel to an outer piece with right sides together, matching the fringe edges. Machine stitch along the length from the neck opening to 4" (10 cm) from the fringe end, leaving an opening at the bottom. Use a skinny seam of 2 picks for your seam allowance. Repeat for the other side, then attached the back center panel to the outer pieces in the same way.

Shoulder darts: With wrong sides out, folded in half at the shoulder, mark the outer edges 2" (5 cm) from the fold with a pin. Mark 2-1/2 (3, 3-1/2, 4)", 6.5 (7.5, 9, 10) cm inward toward the neck opening at the fold. Use the edge of a piece of tape to mark a line between the 2 pin points. Sew the dart from the outer edge to run off the shoulder fold, as shown below. Press the dart toward the back.

Underarm Seam: Mark a point 10" (25.5 cm) down from the dart seam on the outer edges and sew the front and back together at the sides for a length of 4" (10 cm) with a skinny seam.

Your tunic is ready to wear.

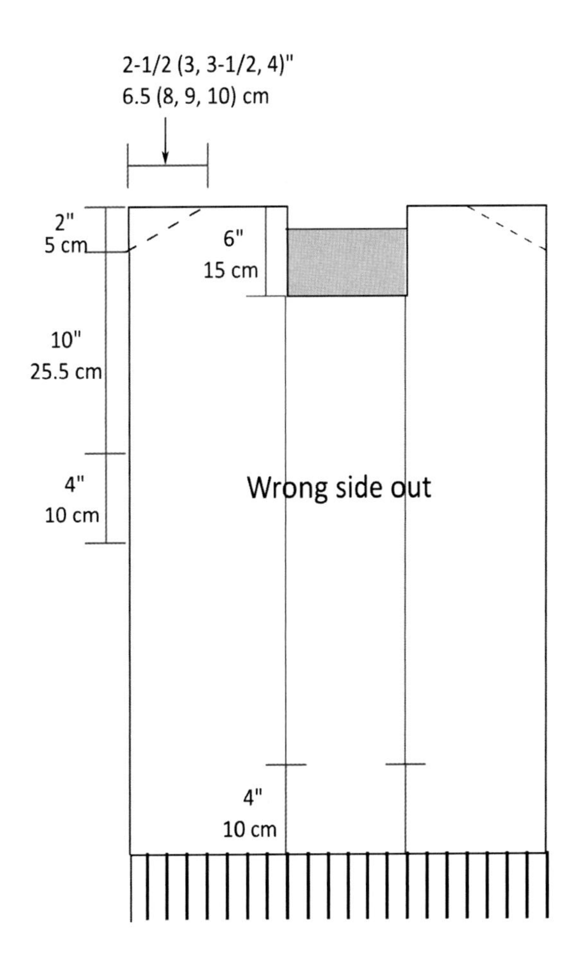

Confetti Scarf **(Make 2 for outer edges of the tunic).**

My 2 scarves for the Upcycled Tunic used different color and choices with the same pattern. One of them changed weft colors as shown at left (optional).

12 epi, 9 ppi

Finished Measurements approx.: 7-1/2 (8-1/4, 9-1/4, 10-1/4)" 18.5 (21, 23.5, 26) cm W x 54" (137 cm) L

Equipment and Materials

- Loom with at least 9"-11" (23-28 cm) weaving width (depending on your size) and a 12 dent reed

Yarn descriptions and Numbering for Charts

#1 = tape – 68 yds (62 m) - a tape or a ribbon yarn that has a flat, woven texture. It is allowed to twist or turn in the weaving. I used Try Lang Lino, 1 ball, 100% linen 50 gm = 120 yds (110 m) or Prism Tencel Tape, 100% Tencel, 1 skein, 2 oz. = 120 yds (109 m)

#2 = fingering gauge, smooth yarn – 213 yds (195 m)– a yarn of consistent roundness that coordinates with the other yarns in solid, tonal or multicolor. I used Mary Gavan Yarns Desert, 50% Organic Cotton, 50% Bamboo, 475 yds (434 m) per skein.

#3 = ladder – 71 yds (65 m) - this adds flecks of jewel tones for the confetti effect. Try EY Novelty Athena, 1 ball, 80% polyester, 20% nylon, 25 gm. = 82 yds or Plymouth Yarn Eros II, 100% nylon, 50 gm = 165 yds (151 m).

#4 = fur – 39 yds (36 m), Prism Plumette , 100% nylon, 2 oz. = 95 yds (87 m). The shorter length of this fur emerges from the woven surface better than a long fur and adds softness and bloom to the scarf.

#5 = Novelty ribbon (optional) - Louisa Harding Lirico,50% Cotton, 28% Acrylic, 22% Polyamide, 100 gm = 262 yds (239 m) . This is a worsted gauge variegated ribbon. I used it to alternate with #2 in the weft for the optional color change you see between the right and left sides, as seen in the photo.

Be inventive with yarn choices. Can't find fur? Try a novelty texture like a thick and thin slub yarn, crepe, or chenille instead. Coordinate colors according to what you can find. The jewel-tone ladder yarn in the warp is the star here for texture.

Advice for Warping

We will alternate 1 strand of novelty yarn with 1 strand of smooth, fine gauge yarn.

The yarns you choose may vary in elasticity. Draw the stretchy loops somewhat loosely as you warp. The non-elastic yarn will end up a couple of inches longer once you wind on, but you can trim it before tying on as there's enough warp to allow. Do your best to smooth the ends for even tension as you tie on. You can correct any unevenness in your fell line after you have woven an inch or so. You simply pull the bow out where any "hills" rise and pull the ties tighter until the fell line straightens, then retie the bow. Loosen the ties where the fell line sinks.

An indirect warp wound on a warping board can minimize excess crossing at the back and should be sleyed according to chart B. If you don't use a warping board, do a direct warp, and start with A.

Warp

8-1/4 (9-1/2, 10-3/4, 12)", 21 (24, 27.5, 30.5) cm W x 86" (219 cm) L = 97 (113, 129, 135) ends, according to A and B below. Warp widths correspond to your tunic size.

The charts are drawn to look like your reed with slots and holes. Chart A is the back of the loom. Chart B is the reverse when you face the front to sley the reed.

Direct Warp: Chart A, from the right, indicates drawing a loop of #1 through a hole, #2 through a slot. Skip a hole and a slot, then draw #3 through a hole, #2 through a slot. Skip a hole and a slot. You'll perform this sequence a total of 5 (6, 7, 8) times as indicated in the green shaded box over the top.

You can continue across with the #2 yarn without cutting and tying off until the end, but you need to tie on, cut, and tie off each of the other yarns to the apron rod every time they appear. Just be careful that #2 goes around the back rod and is placed in the slot to the left of the other yarns each time. Check your work for accuracy every couple of inches.

Continuing left, draw the next sequence 7 (8, 9, 10) times. End with 1 strand of #3*. Tie this one off at the warping peg instead of the back rod. It places the heavier yarn at each selvage - this helps avoid selvages that contract once off the loom due to differential take-up, causing the fabric to sag in the middle.

Chart B: Facing the front of the loom, starting at the right (the single end * stays in place). Sley one of the 2 ends in the first slot into the empty slot to the right. Sley one of the 2 ends in the next hole into the empty hole to its right. Repeat this across until every slot and hole is filled in your warp width This will look like B.

Wind on to the back beam as usual and tie knots and bows onto the front rod to reserve fringe.

Weave

Work in plain weave for 62" (158 cm) alternating one pick of #2 with one pick of #4. If you choose to change the weft shade as I did on one scarf, at 35" (89 cm), switch to one pick of yarn #2 alternating with one pick of yarn #5 for the remaining 27" (68.5 cm).

If you have a problem getting a clean shed opening at any time due to all the yarn variation, place an extra shuttle, warp stick, or pick-up stick in the back shed (behind the reed) to force fibers apart as you weave. Push it to the back beam when not in use.

Remove from the loom, tying 4 strand tassels at each end.

Finish

Wash according to method one on p. 12.

A

7 (8, 9, 10)x | 5 (6, 7, 8)x

*

0 0 0 0 0 0 0 0 0

3 2 3 2 4 2 3 2 1

B

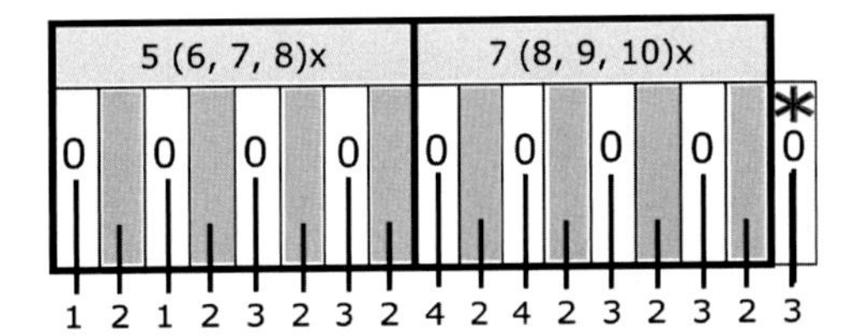

Center Piece Scarf

10 epi, 12-13 ppi

Approximate Finished Dimensions: 5-1/2" (14 cm) W x 49" (125 cm) L

Equipment and Materials

- Loom with at least 7"(18 cm) weaving width
- 10 dent reed
- #1= Short fur yarn like Prism Plumette , 100% nylon , 2 oz. = 95 yds (87 m) or Mary Gavan Yarns Rayon Chenile, 100% rayon, 292 yds (267 m), uses 49 yds (45 m). Use a DK or worsted weight here.
- #2 = Ribbon yarn like Prism Tencel Tape, 100% Tencel or Lang Lino, 100% linen. Uses 85 yds (78 m). This is a tape yarn in DK weight.
- #3 = 1 skein Mary Gavan Yarns Desert, 50% organic cotton, 50% bamboo, 475 yds (434 m). Uses 158 yds (145 m). This is a fingering (5/2) weight.

Warp

6-1/4" (16 cm) W x 79" (200.5 cm) L (62 ends) drawing loops according to the chart below for the number of ends for each yarn, see p. 12, chart reading.

	5x						
2				2		2	1
		2					2
	2		2		2		3

When direct warping, #3 can be carried across without cutting and tying until the end. #1 can be carried for the first 2 loops each time it appears before you cut and tie it to the apron rod. Cut and tie every loop of 2.

I found it easier to draw all of the #3 loops first, leaving every other slot for the other yarns. Then I went back and filled in the #1 and #2 loops.

Weave **(2 pieces)**

with #3 in plain weave for 31" (79 cm), Weave 2 picks with scrap yarn to separate the piece, cutting and tucking ending and beginning weft tails. Weave 25" (64 cm) to complete a total of 56" (143 cm). Cut from the loom, tying 4 strand tassels at each end.

Finish

Wash according to method one, p. 12.

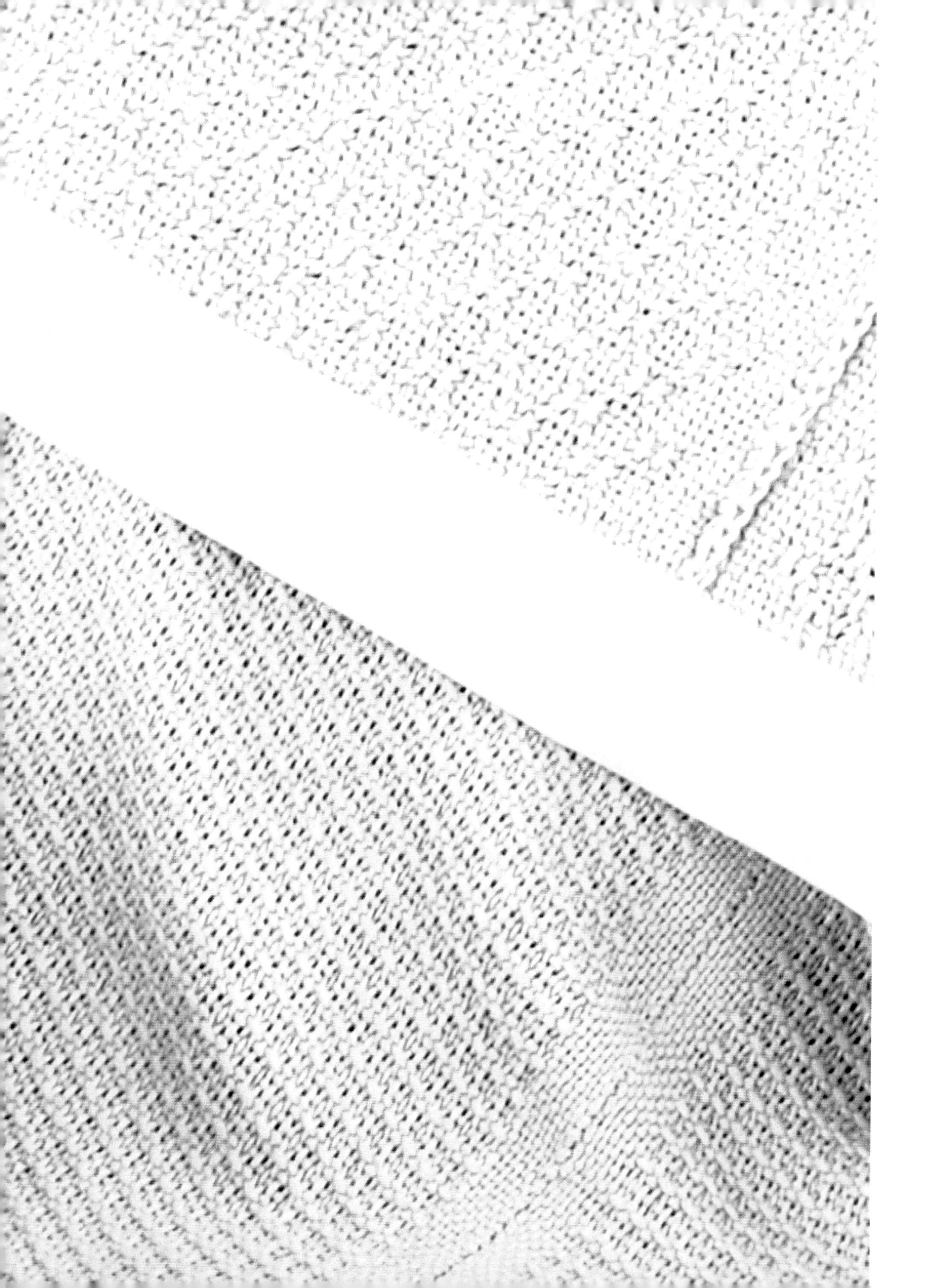

Chapter 9

> **"At the end of the day, it's not about what you have or even what you've accomplished…It's about who you've lifted up, who you've made better. It's about what you've given back."**
>
> **-Denzel Washington**

3 Panel Baby Blankets

There are many ways to make blankets on the little loom. Keeping my focus on simple, I've pared this down to two basic join techniques for a little weave with big results.

My crochet skills are limited, but I found that this method to piece together woven strips with the worsted gauge yarn was easy and fun to do, even if you don't crochet. The finer gauge bamboo was easier to hand sew together using a figure 8 seam.

I've chosen some earth-friendly, machine washable, and affordable yarns that meet the standards for donations to Project Linus if you are so inclined. More on this on p. 171.

Finished Measurements: approximately 36" (91.5 cm) x 36" (91.5 cm)

Equipment

- Rigid heddle loom with at Least 15" (38 cm) weaving width
- 8 dent reed for worsted gauge or 10 dent for DK
- 2 pick-up sticks for Huck Lace, Version 1, 1 pick-up stick for Version 2
- H/8 (5 mm) crochet hook for the slip stitch join (optional, see p. 169)
- 1 package 2" (5 cm) W x 4-3/4 yds (4.35 m) L satin blanket binding. Choose this color before the yarn to make sure it coordinates as available colors may be limited.

- Knit clips to hold the panels together are very helpful.

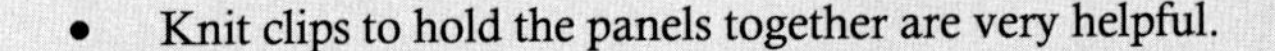

Warp and Weft:

Version 1: 6 skeins Lion Brand Nuboo in Duck Egg, 100% Lyocell, 85 gm = 157 yds (144 m). Uses 837 yds (766 m).

Version 2: 5 skeins Lion Brand Truboo in Lilac, 100% bamboo, 100 gm = 241 yds (220 m). Uses 1127 yds (1031m).

You will warp twice for version 1 or 2, making 2 panels on 1 warp and the 3rd on another.

The bulk of fabric building up on the front beam impedes weaving if you try to weave all 3 panels on one warp. At this time, new devices are coming that allow more fabric build-up on one warp, but they are not universally available yet.

Check your end count and sley left as you warp to get the pick-up patterns to work as instructed. The warp float one and two patterns are interchangeable with either worsted or DK if you follow the widths and end counts for that gauge.

For advice on weaving pick-up patterns, see p. 11. These simple patterns were chosen to make small floats that won't catch on baby toes.

Version 1: **8 epi , 7 ppi (8 dent reed)**

Count and measure carefully as you weave as there will be some matching of the pattern required when you assemble.

Alternately, you can weave this float pattern throughout without concern for matching. Bordering the ends with at least 6 picks of plain weave makes edge finishing easier.

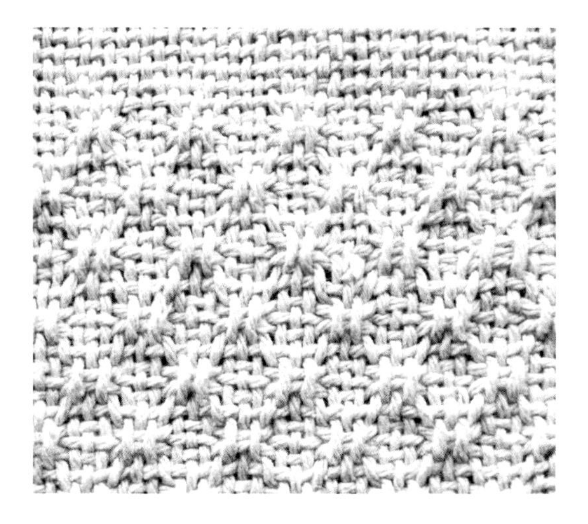

Warp #1: with Worsted

14-1/4" (36 cm) x 101" (257 cm) = 114 ends
Sley the reed to the left.

Set the pick-up stick B: With heddle down, set your pick-up stick behind the reed, skipping over the first 3 ends of the top row, then pick up 2, skip over 2 to the last 4 ends that you will skip over.

Set the pick-up stick A: With heddle still down, behind the reed skip over 5, pick up 2, over 2 to the last 6 ends that you will skip over.

This will leave a plain border.

Weave **(weave 2)**

Proceed according to the chart at right for each of the 2 panels.

Plain	Warp Float
10 picks	
	11" (28 cm)
10 picks	
	11" (28 cm)
10 picks	
	11" (28 cm)
10 picks	

For the warp float sections: You will need to remove pick-up stick A after each 4 step repeat, and place it again before starting another A sequence. B can remain in place throughout. Start with A as follows:

1. Heddle Down
2. Heddle UP and pull the pick-up stick forward
3. Heddle Down
4. Heddle Up

Repeat the sequence with B. When you start at step 1 again, replace A.

Cut and tuck ending and beginning weft tails and separate the panels with 2 picks of scrap yarn to complete the 2nd panel identical to the first.

When you have completed both panels, weave 1/2" (1.5 cm) footer and cut from the loom.

Warp #2:

14-1/4" (37 cm) x 62" (158 cm) = 114 ends

Weave **(weave 1)**

Make one panel identical to the first two.

Finish

Raw finish all ends, p. 18.

Wash the panels according to method one, p. 12, the first time until the raw edges are sealed in the binding. After that, the yarns used wash beautifully in a delicate cycle, cold water, machine wash. Dry flat.

Assemble

Clip 2 panels together using the knit clips. The front and back of these panels are different. Pay attention to getting the right sides together and the pattern to match if you alternated with plain weave.

With the slip stitch or figure 8 join, start 1/2" (1.5 cm) from the edge and join up to 1/2" (1.5 cm) from the end of the panels. This way, you won't stress the raw edges. The blanket binding will cover these gaps.

Flat Slip Stitch Join:

Because cellulosic yarns tend to unply, this join works best with the worsted gauge yarn. If you struggle with this one, the Figure 8 join is easier.

Make a slip knot and place it on your hook.

*Pick up the 1st selvage loop of the piece on your left (through the front).

Pick up the corresponding selvage loop of the piece on the right (through the front).

The working yarn will need to be behind the panels. Place the working yarn over the hook and draw it through all three loops.

Repeat from * to the last loop. Cut the yarn, draw it through the loop, and pull it snug. Weave in the tail.

Figure 8 join: Thread a tapestry needle with yarn. With 2 panels clipped together, attach the sewing yarn to a weft loop at the left panel 1/2" (1.5 cm) above the bottom edge.

*With the needle entering from the underside, pick up the corresponding loop at the right panel selvage. You will be picking up 2 strands (the weft loop and the warp end it surrounds). See the drawing below. When you pull the stitches tight, you will have a nearly invisible seam.

It may be hard to differentiate the loop from the space between the loops on tight selvages. If you start the yarn out right, just count 2 weft picks up from the last loop.

Pick up the next loop from the underside on the left panel and continue from * to the top edge. Tie off and weave in the sewing end, and repeat for the additional panel.

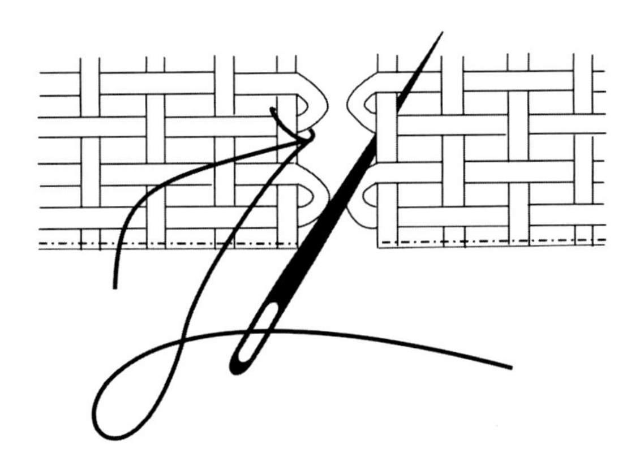

Attach the seam binding: Blanket seam binding comes with one side of the fold shorter than the other to make this easier. If you zigzag effectively along the shorter side, you are sure to catch the other side. This is one process where a video is worth a thousand words so I recommend YouTube.com for the many videos that demonstrate how this is done. I like "Joanne Banko sews a mitered satin binding on a baby blanket."

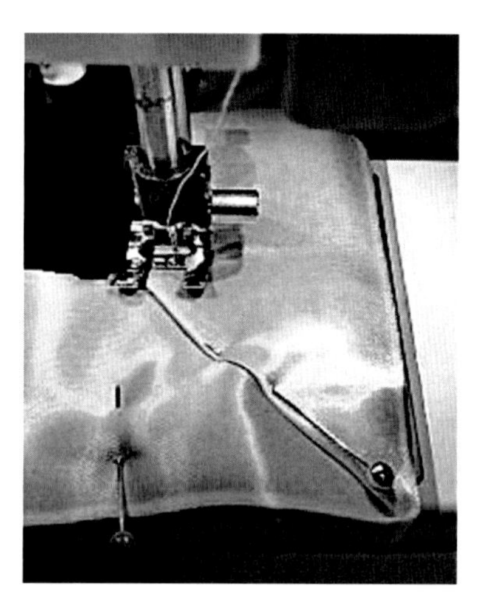

Although she doesn't describe it, sewing on top of the mitered corner shows in her example and is a finish I prefer.

If mitered corners intimidate you, don't forget that you can tuck and square them off as below.

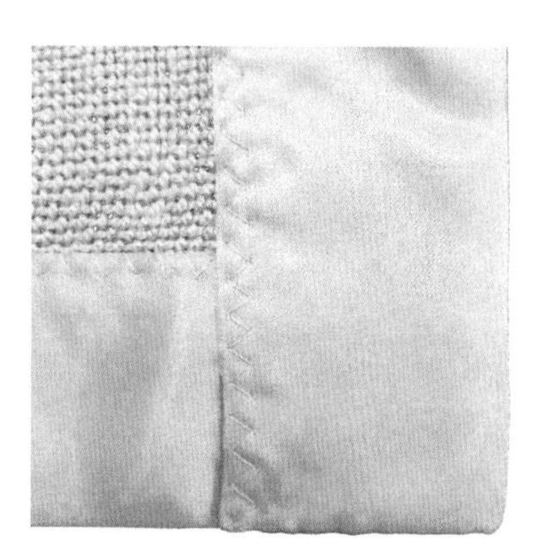

Version 2: **10 epi , 10 ppi (10 dent reed)**

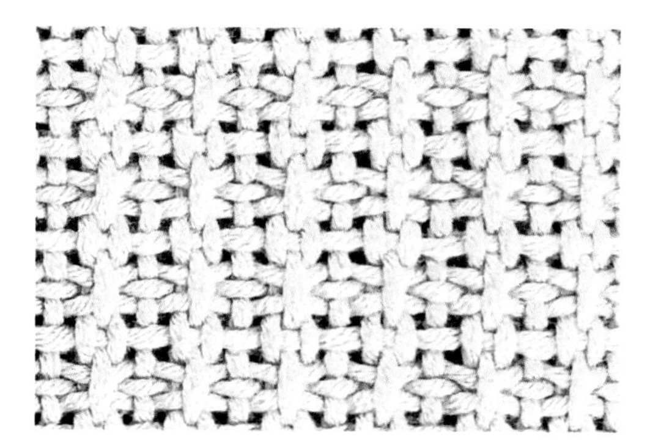

Warp #1: with DK

14-1/2" (37 cm) x 101" (257 cm) = 146 ends
Sley the reed to the left.

Set the pick-up stick: With heddle down, set your pick-up stick skipping over the first 4 ends of the top row, then pick up 1, skip over 1 to the last 4 ends that you will skip over. This leaves a plain border for the warp float.

Weave **(weave 2)**

starting with 6 picks of plain weave, then repeat the warp float sequence that follows:

1. Heddle up and pull pick-up stick forward.
2. Heddle down
3. Heddle up
4. Heddle down

When the first panel measures 38" (96.5 cm), end with step 3 of the pattern, and weave 5 picks of plain weave.

Cut the ending weft tail, weave 2 picks of scrap yarn and complete the 2nd panel identical to the first.

When complete, weave 1/2" (1.5 cm) footer and cut from the loom.

Warp #2:

14-1/2" (37 cm) x 62" (158 cm) = 146 ends

Weave **(weave 1)**

Make one panel identical to the first two.

Finish

as per Version 1. After washing and drying, use the figure 8 join. The slip stitch may be more challenging for the lighter gauge yarn.

Giving Back

Project Linus

From their website, www.projectlinus.org:

HELPING CHILDREN IN NEED

At Project Linus, a non-profit organization, we provide new handmade blankets to children in need. Our blankets are lovingly made by adults *and* children from all walks of life and many different sources.

The organization has chapters throughout the US, where you can find out more about blanket sizes needed.

Key rules to follow for their handmade donations:

No lace, fringe, or animal fibers as these might catch baby toes or irritate sensitive skin, and all contributions must be washable.

Looking for more ways to give back? Www.charitynavigator.org will help you find and validate other worthwhile charitable organizations.

"There is a fountain of youth: it is your mind, your talents, the creativity you bring to life and the lives of the people you love."

Sophia Loren

The work of our hands unites us, rooting us firmly in the present as we focus on process and connecting us deeply with the past as we practice our craft. Most of the fiber artists I know had a mentor from another generation who inspired their work.

My mother started her children on knitting as a way to keep us busy in our early years. Now that she is gone, I still cherish the memories of evenings spent laughing and knitting around her kitchen table many years later. I smile when I remember how she once remarked (in all sincerity), "What do people do who don't knit?" Well, sometimes they weave, mother, and sometimes they do both - and thank you for that.

Don't let anyone tell you that your rigid heddle loom is not a sophisticated tool - only a portal to bigger things. To that, I respond, "Just weave bigger things on your rigid heddle."

Rigid heddle weaving is a noble craft unto itself. It excels in allowing the broad exploration of all that fine yarn offers. The openness of the loom structure and lower working tension allow us the unique benefit to handle the more delicate and varied range of knitting yarns along with weaving yarns. The limitations of size or patterning options are simply a framework to inspire more creativity, as I hope is demonstrated in this book.

As I've said before, creativity is like a muscle. You exercise it, and it rewards you, and as I asked in the exercise at the beginning, "What will you do?"

One last quote to apply to that question:

"Don't bunt. Aim out of the ballpark. Aim for the company of immortals."

- David Ogilvy

I hope this book has helped you aim higher. Please consider reviewing it on Amazon or Goodreads.com.

About the Author:

Tamara Poff weaves, knits, and paints amid the foothills of one of Tucson, Arizona's vast mountain ranges.

With a background in Art Education and Fine Arts, she is the author of *Woven Style for the 15" Rigid Heddle Loom* (2016), and *Color and Texture for the Rigid Heddle Loom* (2019) - books with a focus on taking the weaver " beyond the rectangle" toward new ideas for personal expression. Find these at amazon.com or www.poffstudio.com.

Look for more ideas from Poff Studio at www.youtube.com and online courses for rigid heddle weavers at weavingwithpoffstudio.com.

Little Loom -Think Big

Commissioned pieces made by Tamara Poff for Trice DeWolf Studio Interior Design on behalf of Ocala Eye, Ocala, Florida.

Created on a 15" rigid heddle loom using Schoppel Wolle Gradient and Reggae Solid.

Thoughts on Sustainability

Reclaimed Yarns

I stumbled across a fascinating movement while browsing on Etsy: a new cottage industry for reclaiming yarn by unraveling cast -off sweaters. I bought this gorgeous yarn of cotton and angora blend from Lisa Chimento of Renaissance Yarns.

I was so thrilled about the yarn that I contacted her to find out more about her inspiration.

An avid knitter and crocheter from the age of 8, she discovered spinning at a county fair in her teen years. As a new spinner, she was fascinated with "what's in fiber," devouring every book the library offered on the subject.

When she found two brand name silk sweaters at a yard sale (75 cents apiece), the research and trial and error process to reclaim yarn began. Lisa realized she could produce luxury yarns for pennies, although she admits it's very labor-intensive (apparently a labor of love).

Sadly, she is pausing her shop to attend to personal matters for now, but search "reclaimed yarns" on Etsy.com to find a selection of these unique yarns available from a variety of vendors.

Going Green

All manufacturing poses some environmental risk, whether that is deforestation, pesticide use, or petrochemical contamination. To be "green" is admittedly a matter of being "greener while we work toward better processes.

Acrylic, polyester, and nylon fabrics are, without a doubt, the most toxic to the planet. The lure of their durability, washability, and affordability has made them the "go-to" yarn for baby and budget-minded consumers since their inception, but we are beginning to understand their load on our health and our environment.

Do we really want to wrap a baby in a petroleum product in the first place? Now we learn that these plastics break down into microfibers in the wash that leach into our groundwater and end up in our bodies. But what do we do for washable, wearable, affordable, but less toxic fibers?

We love wool and cotton, but fertilizers, pesticides, water usage, methane contamination...It's mind-boggling, but don't lose hope. Take a look on the internet, and you will find sustainable agriculture explored by sheep growers and cotton farmers alike.

Rayons of bamboo and lyocell (brand name, Tencel) are cellulosic fibers derived from plants but chemically processed. These plants come to our attention due to their robust growth with little or no pesticide or herbicide use. Still, there is the harmful harvesting and processing that is of concern. Tougher scrutiny toward ethical sourcing and closed-loop processing methods to reduce waste show promise to make these the fibers of the future.

I don't think we will ever be without synthetics. Admittedly this book in not 100% synthetic-free, but we can easily move away from them in a big way. For the first time, I want to applaud the efforts of certain discount brands introducing renewable fibers like the ones used in the 3-Panel Baby Blanket, p. 166, as well as an array of recycled fibers.

As a strong supporter of local yarn shops, I suggest you bring these yarns to the attention of the folks at your favorite shop if they don't already carry them, and as always, be a label reader.

Repurposing Yarn Waste

The yarn waste we produce as weavers has been a concern of mine for a while. Some weavers use the scraps for adorning or stuffing hand made dolls. One of my students layered them between sheer fabrics to quilt artful pieces.

I found this fantastic post at www.diyncrafts.com, "50 Cute Projects to Make from Leftover Yarn - They Make Excellent Gifts, Too!"

Save your scraps for kids' projects or local organizations that would welcome them, OR imagine the craft classes you could teach with this material!

Resources

BOOKS AND VIDEOS

Juliet Martin

www.julietmartin.com

-multiple catalogs and art manifestos of her work as a fiber sculptor.

Carol Leigh Brack-Kaiser

www.hillcreekfiberstudio.com

-Continuous Strand Weaving Method, *Nature Provides Dyes for Rainbows,* patterns, and videos.

Jane Dunnewold

www.janedunnewold.com

-multiple books on creative exploration, textile surface design, and on-demand video courses.

Cornelia Tuttle Hamilton

www.hamiltonyarns.com

-multiple patterns and books for knitters.

EQUIPMENT AND MATERIALS

Free Form Cowl

www.darngoodyarn.com
www.interlacementsyarns.com
www.etsy.com

Winter in the Wood Sweater

www.earthguild.com
www.eugenetextilecenter.com (Maurice Brassard)
www.dandoh.com

Patchwork Vest

www.hillcreekfiberstudio.com (continuous strand looms and tools)
www.berroco.com
www.knittingfever.com (Noro)

Folium and Sphere Cowl

www.interlacementsyarns.com
www.janedunnewold.com (Thermofax screens and tools)

Folium and Fairies Wall Hanging

Sources for free photos for transfer:
www.morguefile.com
www.pixabay.com
www.unsplash.com
Search for line drawings or illustrations for many transferable images.

www.urbanoutfitters.com (wooden dowel print hanger)

Trilia Shawl

www.hamiltonyarns.com

Trilia Pillow

www.hamiltonyarns.com
www.knittingfever.com (Noro)

Rayon Ruana

www.interlacementsyarns.com

Open Weave Shawl

ww.etsy.com (handspun yarns)
www.berroco.com (Lang)
www.tahkistacycharles.com
www.spinnery.com (Green Mountain Spinnery)

Bell Sleeve Shrug

www.berroco.com

Urban Shawl

www.hamiltonyarns.com
www.berroco.com
www.diamondyarnusa.com
www.knittingfever.com (Noro)

Houndstooth Tank

www.universalyarn.com
www.interlacementsyarns.com

Confetti Scarf

www.berroco.com (Lang)
www.marygavanyarns.com
www.knittingfever.com (EY Novelties & Louisa Harding)
www.prismyarn.com

Center Piece Scarf

www.prismyarn.com
www.marygavanyarns.com

3-Panel Baby Blankets

www.lionbrand.com